FOOD, FARMING AND RELIGION

Although the religious and ethical consideration of food and eating is not a new phenomenon, the debate about food and eating today is distinctly different from most of what has preceded it in the history of Western culture. Yet the field of environmental ethics, especially religious approaches to environmental ethics, has been slow to see food and agriculture as topics worthy of analysis.

This book examines how religious traditions and communities in the United States and beyond are responding to critical environmental ethical issues posed by the global food system. In particular, it looks at the responses that have developed within Jewish, Christian, and Islamic traditions, and shows how they relate to arguments and approaches in the broader study of food and environmental ethics. It considers topics such as land degradation and restoration, genetically modified organisms and seed consolidation, animal welfare, water use, access, pollution, and climate, and weaves consideration of human wellbeing and justice throughout. In doing so, Gretel Van Wieren proposes a model for conceptualizing agricultural and food practices in sacred terms.

This book will appeal to a wide and interdisciplinary audience including those interested in environment and sustainability, food studies, ethics, and religion.

Gretel Van Wieren is Associate Professor in Religious Studies at Michigan State University, East Lansing, Michigan, USA.

Routledge Environmental Humanities

Series editors: Iain McCalman and Libby Robin

The *Routledge Environmental Humanities* series is an original and inspiring venture recognizing that today's world agricultural and water crises, ocean pollution and resource depletion, global warming from greenhouse gases, urban sprawl, overpopulation, food insecurity and environmental justice are all *crises of culture*.

The reality of understanding and finding adaptive solutions to our present and future environmental challenges has shifted the epicenter of environmental studies away from an exclusively scientific and technological framework to one that depends on the human-focused disciplines and ideas of the humanities and allied social sciences.

We thus welcome book proposals from all humanities and social sciences disciplines for an inclusive and interdisciplinary series. We favor manuscripts aimed at an international readership and written in a lively and accessible style. The readership comprises scholars and students from the humanities and social sciences and thoughtful readers concerned about the human dimensions of environmental change.

FOOD, FARMING AND RELIGION

Emerging Ethical Perspectives

Gretel Van Wieren

LONDON AND NEW YORK

First published 2018
by Routledge
2 Park Square, Milton Park, Abingdon, Oxon OX14 4RN

and by Routledge
711 Third Avenue, New York, NY 10017

Routledge is an imprint of the Taylor & Francis Group, an informa business

© 2018 Gretel Van Wieren

British Library Cataloguing-in-Publication Data
A catalogue record for this book is available from the British Library

Library of Congress Cataloging-in-Publication Data
Names: Van Wieren, Gretel, author.
Title: Food, farming and religion: emerging ethical perspectives/
Gretel Van Wieren.
Description: Abingdon, Oxon; New York, NY: Routledge, 2018. | Series:
Routledge environmental humanities | Includes bibliographical references
and index.
Identifiers: LCCN 2017057474 (print) | LCCN 2018013200 (ebook) |
ISBN 9781315151168 (eBook) | ISBN 9781138557970 (hbk) |
ISBN 9781138557994 (pbk) | ISBN 9781315151168 (ebk)
Subjects: LCSH: Food–Religious aspects. | Food supply–Religious aspects. |
Agriculture–Religioius aspects. | Environmental ethics.
Classification: LCC BL65.F65 (ebook) | LCC BL65.F65 V36 2018 (print) |
DDC 205/.64963–dc23
LC record available at https://lccn.loc.gov/2017057474

ISBN: 978-1-138-55797-0 (hbk)
ISBN: 978-1-138-55799-4 (pbk)
ISBN: 978-1-315-15116-8 (ebk)

Typeset in Bembo
by Deanta Global Publishing Services, Chennai, India

For my parents, Glenn and Jackie Van Wieren, who taught me to love nature.

CONTENTS

Acknowledgments   *viii*

Introduction: thinking ethically about food   1

1   Down on the farm: the historical roots
     of the ecological crisis – agriculture?   21

2   Soil: sacred and profaned   33

3   Plants: the power and miracle of seeds   48

4   Animals: humane, sustainable, spiritual meat?   64

5   Water: precious, polluted, purified   81

6   Climate: religion and food for a hot planet   97

7   The new sacred farm   112

Index   *129*

ACKNOWLEDGMENTS

Several notes of thanks are in order. To the farms that graciously welcomed me into their spaces to learn more about their work: Coastal Roots Farm in Encinitas, California; Mother Carr's Organic Farm in Lynwood, Illinois; Ryan's Retreat in Fort Plain, New York; Rooster Haven Farm in Ghent, New York; Fowler Camp and Retreat Center in Speculator, New York; and Gaining Ground in Concord, Massachusetts – thank you all, for your amazing work. Thanks to Michigan State University for awarding me a Humanities and Arts Research Program Development grant that allowed me to take a semester off teaching and focus on writing. To my colleagues in the Mellon-funded Humanities Without Walls New Ethics of Food project, I am grateful for our far-reaching conversations about food ethics, many of which have influenced my thinking here. Many thanks to my editor, Charlotte Endersby, for her early enthusiasm about the project, and to Leila Walker for guiding me through the publication process. Grateful acknowledgment to the following for permission to reprint previously published material (at times in significantly revised form): *Restored to Earth: Christianity, Environmental Ethics, and Ecological Restoration* published by Georgetown University Press (2013); "Soil as Sacred Religion: The Spiritual Dimensions of Sustainable Agriculture," 2016 Proceedings of the European Society for Agricultural and Food Ethics (EURSafe) published by Wagenigin Academic Publishers; "The New Sacred Farm" published in *Worldviews: Global Religions, Cultures, and Ecology*, 21:2, 2007, 113–33. And to my husband, Jeff Ericksen, and our children, Inga, Clara, and Carl – my inspirations every day.

INTRODUCTION

Thinking ethically about food

In many respects, there is nothing new about the ethical consideration of food and eating. In late antiquity, theologians such as Clement of Alexandria denounced the luxurious, elaborate menus of his age, believing that lavish eating practices denigrated the character of the Christian community. The Rule of Benedict specified that monastic meals should consist of two cooked dishes, apples or vegetables if available, and no meat from the flesh of quadrupeds. In the sixteenth century, the Protestant Reformer John Calvin emphasized the importance of public fasting, admonishing pastors to encourage their congregations to do so during times of social disaster as way to deprecate God's anger.[1]

Yet the questioning about food and eating that goes on today is distinctly different from most of what has preceded it in the history of Western culture. This becomes particularly evident when one looks at the types of worries related to food production and consumption that began to appear in the decades following the Second World War. The Green Revolution, which focused on the research and development of agricultural technologies, raised fundamental questions about global hunger and food production in terms of the extent to which new agrichemical pesticides, herbicides, and fertilizers and breeds of high yield crops were necessary for meeting a growing human population's food needs. The publication of Rachel Carson's *Silent Spring* in 1962 (interestingly published one year prior to the coining of the term "green revolution" by former United States Agency for International Development (USAID) director William Gaud) generated widespread public concern about the potentially deleterious effects of chemical biotechnologies such as DDT on the natural world. The counter-cultural organic foods and anti-hunger movements that developed in the 1960s and 1970s, exemplified in the work of Wendell Berry and Francis Moore Lappé, raised additional questions about industrial agriculture and its relation to the problems of land degradation, global hunger, and, in Berry's terms, "the unsettling of America."

Especially in the past decade, questions related to food production and consumption have intensified as biotechnological developments related to agricultural practices have exploded. The use of recombinant DNA techniques for transforming the genetic basis of agricultural plants and animals has posed significant environmental and ethical questions about which types of alterations are or are not permissible. Questions related to the potential health risks and ecological consequences of genetically modified organisms (GMOs) are now being coupled with debates about intellectual property rights (IPRs) and whether genetically modified (GM) seeds and animals are patentable. Ethical issues of equity and justice are increasingly raised in relation to issues of food access where populations do not have access to healthy and nutritious food, oftentimes due to the social organization of food systems to begin with.

Global environmental issues such as climate change, topsoil and fisheries depletion, land and water pollution, and public health we are fast learning are significantly linked to the agricultural process. Increased global interdependence introduces vexing ethical questions when it comes to analyzing trade-offs related to food's production and consumption, for at times benefits to farmers living in one part of the globe mean losses for poor people living in another part of the world. All of this makes for a dramatically different landscape for exploring questions about food and eating and the moral life than we have found ourselves in the past.

Yet the field of environmental ethics has been slow to see the issues of agriculture and food as topics worthy of analysis. Moreover, where agriculture and food *have* been considered in environmental ethics, religious and spiritual dimensions have been overlooked.[2] This is surprising, particularly when one considers that the academic study of environmental ethics is considered to have formed largely in response to the work of Aldo Leopold and Rachel Carson, both of whom focused on the moral and spiritual implications of industrial agricultural practices in the 1930s and 1960s respectively. Furthermore, the topic of food ethics has become increasingly popular in broader society, including among religious communities, making it even more curious that environmental ethicists have largely overlooked the topic's significance for their task.

Such oversight could be because the professional study of environmental ethics is relatively new, with scholars only being able to cover so many topics in the four decades since its inception. But it may be more than that. Environmental ethics as a field has overwhelmingly focused on developing nonanthropocentric theories of nature's intrinsic or sacred value, to the neglect of considering concrete environmental problems and social practices. Agriculture and food issues have been especially susceptible to such neglect, for there is a strand in modern day environmental thought that views agriculture, along with agriculturally based religions, Abrahamic and Vedic, as the root cause of the ecological crisis.

 The purpose, then, of this book is to examine how religious traditions and communities in the United States and beyond are responding to critical environmental ethical issues posed by the global food system – efforts that I consider part of the growing "food and faith movement." The food and faith movement in the

United States is a loose amalgamation of religious communities and organizations, clergy members and lay volunteers, activists, and agricultural practitioners who are working, in varied and diverse ways, to address the social, ecological, political, and ethical challenges posed by current food systems.[3] Oftentimes these groups work hand-in-hand with secular food and food justice organizations in organizing community-supported agriculture projects, farm to school programs, educational efforts around health, nutrition, cooking, and gardening, and public policy advocacy efforts. What distinguishes religious approaches to this work are the spiritual beliefs, ritual practices, and symbolic meanings that oftentimes orient them. Here, I am most interested in exploring a subset of the food and faith movement, namely, Jewish, Christian, and Muslim groups that are engaged in this work.

I have chosen to focus especially on Abrahamic traditions for several reasons. First, I take a grounded theory approach, which, in this book's case, is attempting to uncover and reveal how contemporary biblical/monotheistic perspectives are being enacted, on the ground (hence grounded theory), in agroecological ways. There are certainly many ways that other spiritual traditions interact with alternative agricultural and food practices in the United States and around the world, and works such as Zeller, Dallam, and Neilson's *Religion, Food, and Eating in North America* (2014) and LeVasseur, Parajuli, and Wirzba's *Religion and Sustainable Agriculture: World Spiritual Traditions and Food Ethics* (2016) speak well to this. Additionally, many farmers, religious or not, see their work as in some sense sacred, even if they are not attached to a specific tradition, signifying that the sacred may for some be found outside of established faith traditions. Such phenomena certainly warrant further investigation. But at least for this book, and this is the second reason I chose to focus on the Abrahamic traditions, it is a matter of scope and need, for while there are numerous books on the intersection of Abrahamic religion, ethics, and the environment few have paid sustained attention to agriculture and food, and none have offered comparative environmental ethical perspectives, as does this book.

As I have already noted, treatments of agriculture and food in contemporary environmental ethics have, over the past several decades, been few and far between. Yet where agriculture and food discussions have developed, they have touched on a dizzying array of topics, from the value of plants, animals, and ecosystems to the relationship between human and biotic health to the role of civic experience in land stewardship to environmental justice. Contributing to this plurality of topics, environmental ethicists have offered mixed sentiments with regard to agriculture's legitimacy as a conservation practice, a topic I address in the following chapter. For now, however, let us examine some of the ways agricultural and food issues *have* been addressed in tandem with environmental concerns, including by academic philosophers, religion scholars and theologians, and popular environmental writers.

Philosophical environmental ethics and food

Among the first contemporary philosophers to seriously consider the topic of agriculture and food were those who approached the issue from the perspective of

First address to food [handwritten annotation]

global hunger, poverty, and social justice. Peter Singer, writing in the 1970s, for example, argued that it was morally indefensible for some of the world's population to live in abundance while others suffered from hunger and starvation.[4] Onora O'Neil and Peter Unger offered equally formative work in the field of hunger ethics which included the volumes, *Faces of Hunger: An Essay on Poverty, Justice, and Development* (1986) and *Living High and Letting Die: Our Illusion of Innocence* respectively (1996). Singer's work on animal welfare too has significantly contributed to the development of agricultural and food ethics, particularly where it has focused on the issue of the moral status of farm animals and the ethics of meat production. His *Animal Liberation: A New Ethics for our Treatment of Animals* (1975) was among the first systematic philosophical analyses of the moral status of nonhuman animals. Singer and Mason's 2006 volume, *The Ethics of What We Eat: Why Our Food Choices Matter*, co-authored with environmental writer and attorney Jim Mason examines the moral consequences of our food choices on others, including fish, chickens, pigs, cows, and farm workers.

Early philosophers writing explicitly on the topic of agriculture and food ethics included Richard Haynes and Paul B. Thompson.[5] In 1982, Thompson became the first philosopher to hold an academic appointment at an agricultural research institution, Texas A&M, where he began to offer regular coursework in agricultural and food ethics. In 1988, Haynes, with the help of the W.K. Kellogg Foundation, a major institutional supporter of the development of the field of agricultural ethics in the 1980s, created the Agriculture Food and Human Values Society (AFHVS) and founded the journal *Agriculture and Human Values*. Also in this year, The European Society of Agricultural and Food Ethics was formed (EURSafe), with its publication, *The Journal of Agricultural and Environmental Ethics*, founded in 2000.

Thompson's work in particular has been influential in making specific connections between agricultural issues and environmental ethics. His now classic volume, *The Spirit of the Soil: Agriculture and Environmental Ethics*, published in 1995, was the first full-length volume to examine agriculture's significance for the conservation movement and for the study of environmental ethics. It evaluated key environmental problems of industrial agriculture, including use of chemical pesticides and biotechnology, as well as dominant philosophies of agriculture – productionism, stewardship, and economics – and their alternative, ecological holism. Thompson (1995) concluded that these models were ultimately inadequate for dissolving the tension between agriculture and environmental ethics. The idea of sustainability, he proposed, provided "some hope" for fostering a newfound spirit of the soil and guiding the goal of agriculture and its reforms. Nevertheless, sustainability should not be seen as a complete or achievable ideal for modern agricultural societies, according to Thompson. Rather it should be understood as an idea "implying a potential but indefinitely deferred ending point," for the dynamics of sustainability itself are defined by incompleteness and reflexivity (1995, 170). Such a position does not reflect modesty, argued Thompson; rather it recognizes the irony and tragedy that come from attempting to pair partial philosophies with elevated ideals.

In *The Agrarian Vision: Sustainability and Environmental Ethics* (2010) Thompson further develops the idea of sustainability, though explicitly within the framework of American agrarian thought. Here Thompson argues that farms, farming communities, and the agricultures that support entire civilizations are excellent models for the complex kinds of ecosocial hybrid systems that need to be sustained if our society is to achieve sustainability at all. Agrarian philosophies, defined by Thompson as "philosophies developed to probe and promote the appropriate relationship between agriculture and the larger society," can help generate the types of questions that are requisite for developing a sustainable society (2010, 1). So too attention to key agrarian principles, namely, that farmers make the best citizens, all politics are local, and self-realization is a community thing, can model ways of thinking about the ethics of people's relationship to land.

Thompson's latest book, *From Field to Fork: Food Ethics for Everyone* (2016) focuses more directly on concrete problems that directly affect real people, animals, and the environment – and in dialogue with a transdisciplinary set of conservation partners. So, for example, Thompson begins with a figure named Dory, who farms and sells the produce she grows at a local farmers market, though she also sometimes sells her neighbor's produce under her stand, even though it is not technically legal to sell another grower's goods under the auspices of one's own. What kind of ethical dilemmas does this raise? wonders Thompson at the book's outset. Thompson repeatedly claims in *From Field to Fork* that he doesn't want to tell his readers what do eat. Yet he does seem to have opinions about certain types of practices that are important for fostering a public food ethics in contemporary culture. These include the enactment of what philosopher Albert Borgmann has termed "focal practices." Focal food practices such as cooking, growing vegetables, cutting wood, and making a fire have historically worked to keep people physically fit, communally connected, and meaningfully engaged. While Thompson does not want to say that people are "ethically obligated to cultivate a performative food ethics around cultural identity construction," he does suggest that "we should engage in these practices, while also being sensitive to the effect that our focal practices might have on others" (Thompson 2016, 45).[6]

Some environmental philosophers have pushed back on Thompson's focus on agrarian thought as a model for sustainable society for its neglect to fundamentally consider issues of justice and fairness.[7] Representing a growing stream within contemporary environmental philosophy, these authors self-identify as "environmental justice philosophers." Some of these philosophers including Kyle Powys Whyte, for example, emphasize the links between *food* and environmental justice, developing a subfield within agricultural and food ethics referred to as food justice studies. The link between food and environmental justice began to be noted in the early 2000s when a special issue of the environmental justice journal *Race, Poverty, and the Environment* highlighted the parallels between the environmental justice movement and some community groups that were focusing on food advocacy issues. In it, the journal's editors proposed that the environmental justice phrase, the environment is "where we live, work, and play," should be reframed to read – the environment is "where, what, and how we eat" (as cited in Gottlieb and Joshi 2010, 4–5).

Food justice-related issues range from consideration of access to safe and healthy food to the benefits and burdens of the food system to animal welfare to farm labor and food work. Scholars and activists draw on various ethical theories and principles to analyze these issues, including rights-based (deontological), welfarist (utilitarian), and tradition-dependent (communitarian). Food justice authors Robert Gottlieb and Anupama Joshi draw on each of these approaches in their book on the emerging food justice movement, *Food Justice* (2010). Food justice, according to Gottlieb and Joshi, 1) ensures "that the benefits and risks of where, what, and how food is grown and produced, transported and distributed, and accessed and eaten are shared fairly" and 2) explicates "what food justice means and how it is realized in various settings," as well as "how food injustices are experienced and how they can be challenged and overcome" (Gottlieb and Joshi 2010, 6).

Even as philosophers such as those just noted have provided a complex of sustainability and justice and ecological and human values examinations, they have neglected other questions central to this book's task. For example: Might the production and eating of food generate certain spiritual experiences and perceptions that intrinsically relate to a sense of moral obligation and responsibility toward land and its beings? Conversely, how are individuals and communities of people shaped and motivated by certain religious beliefs when it comes to food choices? And what types of symbolic meanings and narratives are attached to this or that type of agriculture and eating? These are among the questions that this book engages. For now, we examine how scholars of religion and theology have addressed the issues of agriculture and food, even as they have come relatively recently to the discussion.

Religious environmental ethics and food

As with philosophical approaches, contemporary scholarship in religion and theology on agricultural and food issues began with ethical evaluations of the problem of global hunger. Arthur Simon's 1975 book, *Bread for the World*, for example, titled after the faith-based anti-hunger advocacy organization he founded in the early 1970s, was pivotal in the formation of the field of religious oriented hunger ethics. Simon's work was importantly shaped by biblical narratives that emphasized the moral imperative to advocate on behalf of the poor and oppressed and to feed and clothe the hungry. It emphasized the ethical obligation of all citizens, but particularly people and communities of faith, to engage politically in advocating for public policies that worked to end domestic and global hunger.[8] Christian anti-hunger and poverty activists writing a generation earlier were also significant in the development of theological approaches to hunger ethics. Notable for their attention to community-based farming were Dorothy Day and Peter Maurin, co-founders of the Catholic Worker Movement in the 1930s. Based on their experiences living and working among the homeless poor in New York City, Day and Maurin developed a three-pronged strategy for addressing the problem of poverty and hunger in post-Depression America.[9] This included "hospitality houses" to feed and shelter the hungry poor in the city, the *Catholic Worker* paper, a monthly newspaper that espoused Christian and socialist views on poverty, and, of special interest for this book's purposes, farming communes and agronomic universities (Day 1963, 1983, 1997, 44). The first farming commune developed by Day and Maurin was located on Staten Island, a ferry ride across the harbor from Manhattan. They referred to it as a "garden commune," given its size, which was only about an acre of land behind the house (45).

Contemporary religion scholars and theologians have continued to focus on the social justice aspects of hunger and poverty in their treatment of agricultural and food ethics, yet they have also emphasized additional topics. Christian theologian, Shannon L. Jung (2004), for instance, has examined eating and what he calls "food system disorders," including the various types of eating disorders that have developed in modern societies as well as the "extreme disorder" of global hunger. Jung (2004) considers these issues from the perspective of Christian spirituality and community, proposing ultimately a "new vision for the church" in which food is viewed as a means of revelation and a communal expression of grace. "God intends food and eating to be for the purposes of delight and sharing," writes Jung. "Through eating together we taste the goodness of God" (Jung 2004, 43).

Christian theologian Norman Wirzba too focuses on the biblical and theological significance of food for Christian communities, though focuses more so on the ecological dimensions of the connection between religion and food. In *Paradise of God: Renewing Religion in an Ecological Age* (2003), Wirzba argues that a biblical view of creation can help to provide a holistic view of humanity's place and role in the land community, and serve to correct the conception that Christianity is fundamentally to blame for the current environmental crisis. His 2011 volume, *Food and Faith: A Theology of Eating*, focuses explicitly on the significance of food and eating for Christian theology and faith. Combining trinitarian theological and agrarian philosophical viewpoints, Wirzba emphasizes the sacramental character of eating for Christians. Wirzba echoes Theilhard de Chardin's notion of a Mass on the world to explicate the idea of Eucharistic sacrifice in the context of eating: "Creation is an immense altar upon which the incomprehensible self-offering love of God is daily made manifest…Creation, understood as God's offering of creatures to each other as food and nurture, reflects a sacrificial power in which life continually moves through death to new life" (Wirzba 2011, 126).

Similar to Wirzba's focus on the significance of religious narrative and the agrarian tradition for the problem of modern agriculture, religion scholar Whitney Sanford draws on Hindu and Indian agrarian traditions in her *Growing Stories from India: Religion and the Fate of Agriculture* (2011). Sanford asks: "How does Hindu thought conceptualize the human relationship to the earth in terms of agriculture? And does Hinduism offer strategies to alleviate the social and environmental costs associated with industrial agriculture?" (Sanford 2011, 7). To respond to these questions Sanford looks to narratives of the male agricultural deity, Balaram, who forcibly diverts the Yamuna River goddess to make her waters available to insure agricultural fertility. She also spotlights the springtime festival of Holi, which reminds religionists of the violence that their actions can cause to the larger land community on which they ultimately rely. Sanford stresses the criticality of such alternative agricultural narratives in providing an antidote to the dominant modern industrial agricultural narrative of maximum production at any cost.

In addition to examinations of symbolic meanings and narratives of agriculture and food, scholars of religion and theology have paid significant attention to the issue of the moral status of nonhuman animals. Chief among these has been theologian and Anglican priest, Andrew Linzey. Linzey, who began writing on the topic of animal welfare in the 1970s alongside philosophers Tom Regan and Peter Singer, is perhaps best known for his book *Animal Theology* (1995). In it, Linzey develops a Christian view of animal rights based on a deontological ethic of individual dignity and a theocentric view of creation. He writes: "No human being can be justified in claiming absolute ownership of animals for the simple reason that God alone owns creation" (Linzey 1995, 148). Hunting, meat eating, animal experimentation, and genetic manipulation of animals are unethical, according to Linzey, because each represents the human domination of animals. Genetic engineering of animals, he argues, represents the newest form of domination.[10]

Religious ethicist Anna Peterson too examines the issue of animal welfare in her volume, *Being Animal: Beasts and Animals in Nature Ethics* (2013). Different from Linzey, however, Peterson focuses on the longstanding debate in environmental ethics between animal rights and ecocentrism. While Peterson does not explicitly emphasize food issues, they are nevertheless integrally related to many of the topics she addresses, including the critique made by some environmental thinkers that agriculture represents the "beginning of the end of a healthy relationship with nature" (Peterson 2013, 97). "According to this view domestic animals [are] so embedded in human society that they are no longer part of nature at all but rather coconspirators in humans' assault on the natural world," writes Peterson (97).

Islam scholars Richard Foltz and Sarra Tlili analyze the topic of animal welfare in their *Animals in Islamic Tradition and Muslim Cultures* (2005) and *Animals in the Qur'an* (2012) respectively. Foltz (2005) focuses on the problem of meat eating in Islam, stating that most Islamic environmental environmentalists have advocated against vegetarianism as anti-Islamic. This is because, he writes: "The overwhelming majority of Muslims eat meat; indeed, meat-eating is mentioned in the Qur'an as one of the pleasures of heaven" (Foltz 2005, 25). Islamic environmentalists have favored meat eating uncritically, in Foltz' estimation, in terms of the lack of examination regarding the ecological, social, and dietary effects of animal production and consumption (107–110). Tlili employs a nonanthropocentric examination of just how prevalent animals are in Islamic sacred writings. Even as she includes an interesting discussion on livestock animals her intent is more exegetical than ethical in terms of evaluating contemporary environmental and agricultural problems, as is this book's concern.

Perhaps most resonant with this book's approach is religious education scholar Jennifer Ayers *Good Food: Grounded Practical Theology* (2013) which is based on hands-on experiences teaching hands-on summer courses for high school students at an urban community garden in southwest Atlanta. "In touching the earth in that garden," Ayers writes, "students confronted issues of hunger and nutrition, food policy, environmental justice, and economic disparity. They also, however, experienced a kind of transformation in that garden, a transformation that cries out for theological interpretation and an embodied ecological spirituality" (Ayers 2013, x). Ayers combines this experience-based perspective of environmental justice with structural analysis of the global food system, concluding that "the human, social, and environmental costs of the global food system are great, and are disproportionately borne by the most vulnerable members of our society" (35). The bulk of Ayers' book is spent giving voice to the practices of people and communities of faith, and, in turn, developing a practical theology of food shaped by these voices. "In light of the ongoing challenges of the global food system – despite them, even," writes Ayers, "people of faith are setting a table of resistance, a table of abundance, in the midst of struggle" (158).

Such represent a handful of religious approaches to food and agricultural issues that this book engages and goes beyond. Jung's, Wirzba's, and Sanford's religious agricultural narratives, for example, while instructive for the ethic of eating developed here, do not include analysis of the concrete environmental problems presented by current food systems. Linzey's (1995) and Foltz's (2005) consideration of animal welfare, while ethical in focus, is nevertheless limited by its focus on the moral status of individual animals, to the neglect of consideration of broader ecological dynamics. Ayers states that the community-based farming practices she examines stand in creative tension between concerns for social justice and ecological sustainability, yet this tension points to important ethical questions with regard to the *moral* and *ecological* norms that ought to guide the quest for a sustainable agriculture and for environmental sustainability more generally. Chief among these are debates over what constitutes sustainability itself. These are among the complex set of religious and ethical issues that will be addressed in subsequent chapters. Yet additional treatments of the environmental ethical elements of agriculture and food must be noted as well.

Agricultural and food writing and environmental ethics

Beyond professional philosophers, religion scholars and theologians, several authors are notable for their contributions to the development of agricultural and food ethics, including its spiritual and moral dimensions. Perhaps more than any other contemporary writer, American essayist and poet, Wendell Berry has popularized farming's values-based conservation potential. Berry's work, beginning most notably with his 1977 classic, *The Unsettling of America: Culture & Agriculture*, is highly critical of industrial agriculture and the type of food and eating it has engendered in modern society. This model of agriculture and eating, Berry argues, has been shaped by a mentality of exploitation that is deeply rooted in America's past of conquest and victimization. Though the actors and practices over time have changed – Cortes' time was one of conquerors and victims; ours is one of exploitation and nurturers, states Berry – the current environmental crisis, reflected paradigmatically in agricultural practice, remains ultimately a crisis of character, a disease of our minds and values.

We can depict the strip miner as model exploiter, suggests Berry, and the old-fashioned farmer as model nurturer. He writes:

> The exploiter is a specialist, an expert; the nurturer is not. The standard of the exploiter is efficiency; the standard of the nurturer is care. The exploiter's goal is money, profit; the nurturer's goal is health – his land's health, his own, his family's, his community's, his country's. Whereas the exploiter asks of a piece of land only how much and how quickly it can be made to produce, the nurturer asks a question that is much more complex and difficult: What is its carrying capacity? (That is: How much can be taken from it without diminishing it? What can it produce dependably for an indefinite time?)
>
> *(Berry 1977, 7)*

Berry proposes small-scale family and community-based farming as an alternative to large-scale industrial agriculture. This is because industrial agriculture alienates eaters from farming and from developing a sense of relationship with the land, which, in turn, disallows them from understanding eating as an agricultural, as well as a sacramental act.

"The industrial eater," Berry writes, "is, in fact, one who does not know that eating is an agricultural act, who no longer knows or imagines the connections between eating and the land, and who is therefore necessarily passive and uncritical – in short, a victim" (Berry 1989, 146). Moreover, such forgetfulness about the intrinsic relationship between eating and the land can further disable people's capacity for developing an ecological consciousness. Farming and eating for Berry represent spiritual and moral practices through which people may reflect upon and enact their vocation as citizens of creation. "To live," writes Berry, "we must daily break the body and shed the blood of Creation. When we do this knowingly, lovingly, skillfully, reverently, it is a sacrament. When we do it ignorantly, greedily, clumsily, destructively, it is a desecration. In such desecration we condemn ourselves to spiritual and moral loneliness, and others to want" (Berry 1981, 281).

Other writers who have emphasized the spiritual and moral significance of agriculture and eating include Indian physicist and environmental writer and activist Vandana Shiva. Shiva, who won the Alternative Nobel Peace Prize (the Right Livelihood Award) in 1993, is considered the agrarian mind of the global South, as well as of ecofeminist thought. Building on India's longstanding agrarian tradition, Shiva cites the role that the subcontinent played in shaping the thought of organic agriculture's founder, Sir Albert Howard. Howard, a botanist by training, was sent to Patna, Bihar by the British Empire in 1905 to improve Indian agriculture. When he arrived in the peasant neighborhood of Pusa, however, he found thriving crops that were virtually free of disease, without use of pesticides. Howard decided that he "could not do better than watch the operations of these peasants and acquire their traditional knowledge as rapidly as possible" (as cited in Shiva 2011, foreword to Sanford 2011). Based on his observations of Indian peasant farmers, Howard went on to teach the West and the world about sustainable and organic farming methods.

Shiva argues that, "an agriculture of permanence grows out of a sacred relationship with the earth" (foreword). She, along with Berry, is deeply critical of Western industrial agriculture and the globalization of large-scale farming operations and techniques. Shiva also views eating as an agricultural, and a spiritual and moral, act. Drawing on India's religious traditions, Shiva writes that the act of growing and giving food in abundance is the highest *dharma* or spiritual and moral duty. She cites the sacred text, the *Taittiriya Upanishad*:

> From food [anna], verily, creatures are produced
> Whatsoever [creatures] dwell on the earth.
>
> For truly, food is the chief of beings....
>
> Beings here are born from food, when born they live by food, on deceasing they enter into food.
>
> Food is alive, it is not just pieces of carbohydrate, protein and nutrient, it is a being, it is a sacred being.
>
> Verily, they obtain all food
> who worship Brahma as food.
>
> *(As cited in Shiva 2011, foreword to Sanford 2011)*

Shiva continues: "When agriculture is a sacred duty for maintaining life on earth, the seed is sacred, the soil is sacred, the cow is sacred, and the trees are sacred" (foreword). Drawing on this sacred view of agriculture, Shiva founded the organization Navdanya, a network of seed keepers and organic producers in India. Meaning "nine seeds" and "new gift," the organization's name symbolizes protection of biological and cultural diversity and promotion of the idea of seeds as commons. "Conserving seed is conserving biodiversity," states Navdanya's, "conserving knowledge of the seed and its utilization, conserving culture, conserving sustainability."[11]

Along with Berry and Shiva, American agronomist Wes Jackson has been a pioneer in promoting sustainable agriculture and its spiritual and moral dimensions. Jackson, as with Berry and Shiva, began his career in academia, leaving to return to his home state of Kansas to farm and write. In 1976, Jackson founded *The Land Institute*, which he still runs, a research center devoted to developing what Jackson calls "natural systems agriculture" or perennial polyculture. The type of agriculture that Jackson envisions uses nature as its model, and is characterized by developing and integrating new breeds of perennial crops, such as sunflower, sorghum, and wheat, that reseed themselves rather than requiring annual replanting and nitrogen input. This type of perennial agriculture promotes an ongoing and mutually beneficial relationship between plants and soil, argues Jackson, causing less erosion and soil depletion than modern methods of annual cropping.

It also can promote a healthier relationship between people and land, according to Jackson. The ecological ethic that undergirds such an agricultural model should be embraced, Jackson argues, as part of America's Christian heritage. In his classic book, *New Roots for Agriculture*, Jackson spells out this argument in his chapter "The Religious Dimension," writing:

> I believe that Blake and Gandhi are both correct. Humans must and will have some religion and it is best to work it out in the context of our own cultural and religious heritage. For Western Civilization, that is the Judaeo-Christian heritage, and what it has to offer is rich and filled with hope. It is a tradition that has allowed for an extension of myths so that they may more fully embrace newly perceived realities. The new truth of one creation shows that all species are in it together, that what affects one affects all. Furthermore, there is no environment 'out there' consisting of 'nothing but' objects. The nonliving world eventually becomes a part of us.
>
> *(Jackson 1980, 1985, 73)*

Jackson cites Aldo Leopold to accentuate his point about the need to work out a land ethic in the context of religion. The adoption of a new societal land ethic, wrote Leopold, will ultimately require "an internal change in our intellectual emphasis, loyalties, affections and convictions," a change which can only evolve in the mind of a thinking community" (72–73).

Berry, Shiva, and Jackson have written about the role and significance of certain spiritual and moral values in developing a culture of land marked by a more sustainable and just food system. Yet these accounts have only partially explored the types of religious perceptions, beliefs, practices, and experiences that are embedded in the emergent food and faith movement. Further, the scope of their work precludes consideration of the plural ways in which religious narratives and traditions may relate to understandings of food and eating. Throughout this book I critically probe each of the above perspectives on agriculture, eating, environmental ethics, and spirituality. As will become evident as my argument develops, I also take these treatments in different directions, especially in terms of the types of communities, experiences, and values I explore with regard to the whole food process. Much more needs to be said about the question of the meaning of agriculture and food, a task I undertake in the chapters that follow. Next, however, an additional preliminary step is needed. For even as the spiritual and moral dimensions of agriculture and food have been addressed in various ways in the agriculture and food literature, the point remains that food ethics' religious aspects and implications have not been considered systematically and explicitly in the dominant work in the field. Thus, in this section I define, however briefly, the categories "religious" and "ethical," as well as the correlative terms "spiritual and "moral," given their centrality throughout this project.

Defining "religion," "spirituality," "ethics," and "morality"

In contemporary parlance, spirituality is generally contrasted with religion: that is, spirituality is viewed as personal and subjective and religion is understood as institutional and dogmatic. This is evident, for example, in the popular sentiment, "I am spiritual but not religious." Sociologists like Wade Clark Roof tend to accept this distinction, as in: "to be religious conveys an institutional connotation [while] to be spiritual ... is more personal and empowering and has to do with the deepest motivations in life" (Roof 1993, 75–76).

Religion and spirituality need not, however, be viewed only in opposition. Both may be viewed, as they are in this work, as arising from the inherent human impulse to make sense of and find meaning in relation to life's "big questions," including the mysteries, wonders, and beauties of the universe and of Earth. Although spirituality may be "less oriented to a fixed creed or defined denomination, [and] more committed to the long path toward spiritual truth," this very path, for some, is to be found within the deepest truths of the world's major religious traditions (Gottlieb 2007, 149). For example, religious writings for thousands of years have addressed the ways in which religion has fostered deep experiences of transcending the conventional self and social norms, communing with the divine or Ultimate Reality in the universe, and feeling a sense of awe, amazement, and wonder in relation to world around oneself (149).

Within the religion and ecology field, the concept of "religion," rather than "spirituality," is generally used to refer to nature oriented spiritual–religious phenomena. Mary Evelyn Tucker and John Grim and Bron Taylor, for example, similarly use the term "religion" in their primary definitions of earth-based religiosity – "religious ecology" and "nature-as-sacred-religion" respectively – despite the fact that Tucker and Grim focus on analysis of the major global religious traditions, and Taylor emphasizes nontraditional and emergent religious activities.

Further, both Tucker's and Grim's and Taylor's concepts of nature religion include similar elements. For example, each includes the idea that a religious understanding of the human–nature relationship includes an element of deep connection or kinship between human and nonhuman beings. A "religious ecology," according to Tucker and Grim, is characterized by an "awareness of kinship with and dependence on nature for the continuity of all life" (2001); "nature-as-sacred-religion," believes Taylor, involves the idea that humans are "bound to and dependent upon the earth's living systems" (2007: 867). Moreover, concepts of nature religion such as the ones just cited tend to involve the idea that the human connection with the natural world can foster positive transformation and healing, as well as a deep sense of meaning, satisfaction, and fulfillment. Insofar as nature is understood as in some sense sacred or holy it is also viewed as "worthy of reverent care" (Taylor 2007, 867). Conversely, in the understandings of nature religion just mentioned, "damaging nature is considered to be an unethical and desecrating act" (867).

As with the notions "religion" and "spirituality," the concepts "ethical" and "moral" are commonly distinguished. "Morality," like "spirituality," tends to be associated with concrete experience and action, whereas "ethical," like "religion," tends to refer to a systematic approach to morality (in religion's case, a systematic and often institutional approach to spirituality). Morality tends therefore to refer to matters of individual human choice and character, while ethics tends to refer to a set of principles or a systematic framework for stipulating what constitutes right or good action, modes of being, or outcomes.

This said, there is no consistent differentiation between "moral" and "ethical" in the ethical literature, and I too tend to use the terms interchangeably. Still, if a distinction is made between moral and ethical, I tend to follow the difference just noted – that is, I use "ethics" and "ethical" to refer to a systematic approach to morality ("environmental ethics"), and "moral" and "morality" to refer to the experience involved with deciding to act in this or that way or to be this or that type of person ("ecological morality"). Similarly, if a distinction is made between religion and spirituality, I tend to use "religion" and "religious" to refer to a systematic approach to spirituality (Jewish/Christian/Muslim-supported agriculture projects as "religious farming"), and "spirituality" and "spiritual" to refer to concrete experiences or action ("land-based spiritual experience").

Considering a comparative religious environmental ethical approach to food

The approach I use in this book is best thought of as "religious ethics," and more specifically "comparative religious environmental ethics," given my attention to multiple faith traditions and environmental issues. I use the term "environmental ethics" to include both philosophical and religious approaches, though where a distinction is made I use the terms "philosophical environmental ethics" and "religious environmental ethics," as well as "environmental philosophy" and "environmental theology." Throughout the book, I use the terms "food ethic," "environmental food ethic," and "religious environmental food ethic" to refer to an environmental ethic developed specifically with agricultural and food practices in mind.

My approach to food ethics in this book may also fall under the heading "religion and "ecology/nature." I use the category "ecology/nature" because the two main schools of thought within religious studies that deal with environmental issues refer to themselves as scholars of "religion and ecology" (Mary Evelyn Tucker and John Grim) and "religion and nature" (Bron Taylor). I draw on both of these approaches to the study of religion and ecology/nature in the new food ethic constructed in this book. While I examine faith communities associated with major religious traditions (Tucker and Grim's approach), I also examine spiritual elements embedded in the ethical food movement, and the fundamental experience of the human connection to nature that food production and consumption activities may yield (Taylor's approach).

In both cases I employ a religious ethics framework that I would call eclectic and interdisciplinary, amalgamating various religious approaches under the rubric of comparative religious ethics and, most broadly, the environmental humanities.

Different from most comparative environmental ethical treatments, this book focuses on concrete environmental entities and issues – soil, plants, animals, water, climate – as the comparative foothold, examining how different faith traditions and groups are responding to critical problems in food and agriculture associated with such environmental implications. The book weaves consideration of human well-being and justice throughout, though its focus is on how the total food process – from production to distribution to consumption to waste – impacts nonhuman organisms and natural processes and systems. Topics include land degradation and restoration, genetically modified organisms and seed consolidation, animal welfare, water use, access, pollution, and climate. In the end, I propose a model for concep-tualizing agricultural and food practices in sacred terms.

Industrial versus restorative agriculture

A final definitional step is in order, given how this book juxtaposes current indus-trial agricultural practices with smaller-scale sustainable ones, based on the fact that the latter is the type of food and farming work most often promoted and practiced by those in the food and faith movement. Even as there is no standard defini-tion of what is commonly referred to as "industrial agricultural" –also sometimes called "conventional agriculture," "corporate agriculture," and "large-scale agricul-ture" – there are basic features that many individuals and groups working in the food and faith movement routinely critique. These include, for instance, industrial agriculture's emphasis on "rapid technological innovation; large capital investments in order to apply production and management technology; large-scale farms; sin-gle crops/row crops grown continuously over many seasons; uniform high-yield hybrid crops; extensive use of pesticides, fertilizers, and external energy inputs; high labor efficiency; and dependency on agribusiness" (USDA 2007).

Alternatively, the types of agricultural systems that Berry, Shiva, and Wirzba pro-pose, as already noted, designate what Sanford has called "a set of agricultural practices that are deliberatively different from what today is considered conventional agricul-ture; alternative agricultures include, but are not limited to, organic agriculture, eco-logical agriculture, agroecological restoration, and agroecology" (2011, 16–17). These approaches involve a range of agricultural models, yet they share crucial features, such as a reliance on the ecological concepts of balance, stability, and interdependence. Taken together, I will throughout this book refer to these types of alternative agri-cultural practices as "restorative agriculture." Restorative agriculture as I understand it strives to support a range of social and ecological values, from human health and well-being to animal welfare, biodiversity, and ecological integrity.[12] Additionally, restora-tive forms of agriculture emphasize the role that food and farming activities can have on connecting people to the Earth in ways that are meaningful, fulfilling, and just, as well as in ways that engender a sense of care and respect for the land and its beings. Long-term environmental sustainability may be considered the lodestar of restorative agricultural efforts, yet the regeneration of degraded lands and the empowerment of struggling communities is the more immediate goal.

The outline of the chapters

I do not claim in this book to construct a fully comprehensive religious food ethic; rather, the ethic developed in the pages that follow is largely limited to a consideration of agriculture and food in the West, as well as to a treatment of the Abrahamic traditions, as already noted. This does not, of course, necessarily preclude its potential relevance for other contexts and traditions, though it does limit the types of sources that are drawn upon, and, in turn, the sets of the questions that these sources help to form. Further, the religious food ethic developed in this volume does not claim to cover all of the critical ethical issues in agricultural/food or environmental ethics, even as it does attend to the major themes that a more comprehensive food ethic will need to address – the themes, for example, of the value of nature, norms of social ecological community, and virtues of human ecological identity – it does not claim to treat these themes exhaustively or definitively.

Even as I am trained primarily as a Christian ethicist, I have taught Religious Studies for the past eight years at a large public university where my courses focus on comparative religion, ethics, and the environment. I am not, in other words, writing in this book as a Christian theologian or from within that tradition to change it, even as I do work from a Christian–Western philosophical and religious ethical base. Christianity does receive more attention than Judaism or Islam, though this mostly has to do with the fact that much more has been written on Christian environmental/food/agricultural ethics than the other Abrahamic traditions, even as the Jewish food movement is arguably the most active in the United States.[13] The more significant point, in my mind, is that food is one of those topics that is especially ripe for transdisciplinary, transreligious examinations within the environmental humanities, and this book falls into that intersection. Further, the book provides a kind of test case and method for doing the kind of comparative religious ethics based on concrete environmental problems detailed above, an untapped approach both within the study of comparative religious and environmental ethics.

The more modest task of this book, then, is to develop a guide or a framework for an environmental ethic that is explicitly shaped by food and agricultural thought in Jewish, Christian, and Islamic traditions. To this end, Chapter 1 examines various ways that agriculture has been viewed in environmental ethics, including key critiques of agriculture as the root cause of the ecological crisis as evidenced in the argument famously put forward by Lynn White, Jr. Chapter 2 conversely explores ways in which soil is viewed as sacred in the history of the sustainable agriculture movement by examining the work of some of its central thinkers, including Rudolf Steiner, Liberty Hyde Bailey, and George Washington Carver. Chapters 3 through 6 continue this constructive exploration, beginning with an examination of religious responses to GMOs (Chapter 3). Chapter 4 compares the variety of ways in which eating animals has been treated in contemporary Jewish, Christian, and Muslim ethics, highlighting the role that some religious farms are playing in producing ecologically sustainable meat. Chapter 5 explores the issue of global water usage for agriculture, and the impact of current farming practices on water quality in the United States and abroad. In Chapter 6, we consider how agriculture is impacting global climate change, and the extent to which religious traditions are acknowledging the problem of agriculture in faith statements on climate change. The final chapter (7) explicates meanings for the production and eating of food based on the work of three religious farms that view agriculture as both a symbolic, ritual activity, as well as a practical, ecological one.

The method and organization of the book attempt to speak to the environmental impacts of the total food process from the ground up – from soil to plants to animals to water to climate – as well as how engagement with agricultural and food work in each of these areas can generate positive environmental spiritual and moral values. Overall, I argue that the approaches to food and agricultural issues enacted by the religious groups highlighted in this book can provide a promising model for the nature–culture relation, one that ought to shape twenty-first-century environmentalism as well as environmental ethics. I further argue that the explicit treatment of food and agriculture as an ethical framework may push the field of religious environmental ethics in a more action oriented, experience-based direction, deepening our understanding of the way in which particular environmental activities may shape certain spiritual and moral values. Focusing specifically on a lived environmental activity such as agriculture and the concrete experiences it can yield, may also helpfully illuminate resources within Jewish, Christian, and Islamic traditions that speak to the human relationship to land. Ultimately, agriculture's grounding in both agroecological science and practical experience provides a distinctive context for examining the paradoxical relationship between scientific and religious, secular and sacred ways of knowing about the natural world.

Notes

1   For an excellent overview of these examples as well as a medieval history of Christian eating practices, see David Grumett and Rachel Muers' *Theology on the Menu* (London: Routledge, 2010).
2   Consider the topics addressed at the annual meetings of the two largest professional societies dedicated to the scholarly study of agricultural and food ethics – the Agriculture, Food and Human Values Society (AFHVS) and the European Society for Agricultural and Food Ethics (EURSafe). Of the hundreds of papers given at the 2014–15 meetings, both of which I attended, only one or two related in any way to the topic of religion or spirituality. This is too bad, I want to argue in this book, for the very act of producing and eating food and the organization of the food system itself provokes critical questions that increasingly elicit spiritual and moral responses from religious and secular communities alike.
3   To my knowledge, there are no empirical studies on the number of religious congregations and organizations in the United States currently involved in food ethical issues. A number of recent books present ethnographic and case study-based work on the food and faith movement in America, including, for example, Fred Bahson's *Soil and Sacrament: A Spiritual Memoir of Food and Faith* (2013), Jennifer Ayers' *Good Food: Grounded Practical Theology* (2013), and Benjamin Zeller, Marie W. Dallam, Reid L. Neilson et al., ed. *Religion, Food, and Eating in North America* (2014).
4   Peter Singer, "Famine, affluence, and morality," *Philosophy and Public Affairs*, vol. 1, no. 3 (Spring 1972): 229–243.

5 Additional philosophers working on the topic of agriculture early on were Jeffrey Burkhardt and Stanislaus Dunden. Burkhardt, writing in the 1980s, was invited to be part of a research group at the University Kentucky with sociologists, Lawrence Busch and William Lacy, who, along with Frederick Buttel, had written extensively on agriculture and political economy. University coursework in agricultural ethics began to be regularly offered in the early 1980s by Dunden and Thompson, as well as by the agronomist Thomas Ruehr and the economist Alan Rosenfeld. For this historical sketch, I am indebted to Paul B. Thompson's excellent overview, "Agricultural Ethics" (2014).

6 As an aside, let me say as an ethicist trained in religious studies that I appreciate the fact that Thompson acknowledges in his work the role that ritual and symbolic activities play, for better or worse, in the formation and performance of values, virtues, and norms in relation to the production and eating of food. Thompson even goes as far to say that the "give and take between symbolic projection and material performance instantiates what we mean by an ethic in the broadest and deepest sense" (Thompson 2016, 43).

7 See, for example, Anthony, R. (2010) "Author meets critics panel: Paul B. Thompson's (2010) The Agrarian Vision: Sustainability and Environmental Ethics" in *Journal of Agricultural Environmental Ethics* 25, 499–501.

8 Over the intervening decades, Bread for the World has initiated anti-hunger public advocacy campaigns on a far-ranging set of agriculture and food related policies, from Supplemental Nutrition Assistance Program (SNAP, formerly food stamps) to United States food aid programs (Arthur Simon (1975) *Bread for the World*).See also Arthur Simon (2009) *The Rising of Bread for the World: An Outcry of Citizens against Hunger* and David Beckmann and Arthur Simon (1999) *Grace at the Table: Ending Hunger in God's World*.

9 "Poverty is a strange and elusive thing," wrote Day. "I have tried to write about it, its joys and its sorrows, for thirty years now; and I could probably write about it for another thirty without conveying what I feel about it as well as I would like. I condemn poverty and I advocate it; poverty is simple and complex at once; it is a social phenomenon and a personal matter. Poverty is an elusive thing, and a paradoxical one." See Dorothy Day, *Loaves and Fishes* (1963, 1983, 1997, 71).

10 Christian theologian, Stephen Webb focuses less on ethical analysis of the status of animals, and more on a Christian historical analysis of whether Christians should eat meat. He argues that a biblical view of animals provides an alternative to animal rights' and holistic environmental theological perspectives, both of which elide certain conceptual boundaries according to Webb. See Stephen H. Webb, *Good Eating* (2001).

11 See Navdanya website, www.navdanya.org/ (accessed on January 13, 2014).

12 On the range of values sustainable agriculture fosters, see Paul B. Thompson's "Sustainable agriculture: What it is and what it is not," *International Journal of Agricultural Sustainability* (2007).

13 Nigel Savage, founder of Hazon, likely the largest Jewish and other religious food organization in the world, pointed this out to me. Personal communication, July 7, 2014.

References

Anthony, R. (2010) "Author meets critics panel: Paul B. Thompson's (2010) The Agrarian Vision: Sustainability and Environmental Ethics" in *Journal of Agricultural Environmental Ethics* 25, 499–501.

Ayers, J.R. (2013) *Good Food: Grounded Practical Theology*, Baylor University Press, Waco, TX.

Bahson, F. (2013) *Soil and Sacrament: A Spiritual Memoir of Food and Faith*, Simon & Shuster, New York, NY.

Berry, W. (1977) *The Unsettling of America: Culture and Agriculture*, Sierra Club Books, San Francisco, CA.

Berry, W. (1981) "The gift of good land," in Berry, W. *The Gift of Good Land: Further Essays Cultural and Agricultural*, North Point Press, New York, NY.

Berry, W. (1989) "The pleasures of eating," in Berry, W. (2010) *What Are People For?*, Nortn Point Press, New York, NY.

Day, D. (1963, 1983, 1997) *Loaves and Fishes: The Inspiring Story of the Catholic Worker Movement*, Orbis, Maryknoll, NY.

Foltz, R. (2005) *Animals in Islamic Tradition and Muslim Cultures*, Oneworld Publications, Oxford.

Gottlieb, R. and Joshi, A. (2010) *Food Justice*, MIT Press, Cambridge, MA.

Gottlieb, R.S. (2007) *A Greener Faith: Religious Environmentalism and Our Planet's* Future, Oxford University Press, London.

Grumett, D. and Muers, R. (2010) *Theology on the Menu: Asceticism, Meat, and Christian Diet*, Routledge, London.

Jackson, W. (1980, 1985) *New Roots for Agriculture*, University of Nebraska Press, Lincoln, NE.

Jung, S.L. (2004) *Food for Life: The Spirituality and Ethics of Eating*, Fortress Press, Minneapolis, MN.

Le Vasseur, T., Parajuli, P. and Wirzba, N. eds. (2016) *Religion and Sustainable Agriculture: World Spiritual Traditions and Food Ethics*, University of Kentucky Press, Lexington, KY.

Linzey, A. (1995) *Animal Theology*, University of Illinois Press, Urbana, IL.

O'Neil, O. (1986) *Faces of Hunger: An Essay on Poverty, Development*, Allen & Unwin, London.

Peterson, A.L. (2013) *Being Animal: Beasts and Animals in Nature Ethics*, Columbia University Press, New York, NY.

Roof, W.C. (1993) *A Generation of Seekers*, Harper, San Francisco, CA.

Sanford, W. (2011) *Growing Stories from India: Religion and the Fate of Agriculture*, University of Kentucky Press, Lexington, KY.

Shiva, V. (2011) "Foreword" to Sanford, W. (2011) *Growing Stories from India: Religion and the Fate of Agriculture*, University of Kentucky Press, Lexington, KY.

Simon, A. (1975) *Bread for the World*, Paulist Press, New York, NY.

Simon, A. (2009) *The Rising of Bread for the World: An Outcry of Citizens against Hunger*. Paulist Press, New York, NY.

Singer, P. (1975) *Animal Liberation: A New Ethics for our Treatment of Animals*, New York Review/Random House, New York, NY.

Singer, P. (1996) *Justice* and *Living High and Letting Die: Our Illusion of Innocence*, Oxford University Press, New York, NY.

Singer, P. and Mason, J. (2006) *The Ethics of What We Eat: Why Our Food Choices Matter*, Rodale Books, Emmaus, PA.

Taylor, B.R. (2007) "Focus introduction: Aquatic nature religion," *Journal of the American Academy of Religion* 75(4), 863–74.

Thompson, P.B. (1995) *Spirit of the Soil: Agriculture and Environmental Ethics*, Routledge, London.

Thompson, P.B. (2007) "Sustainable agriculture: What it is and what it is not," *International Journal of Agricultural Sustainability* 5(1), 5–17.

Thompson, P.B. (2010) *The Agrarian Vision: Sustainability and Environmental Ethics*, University of Kentucky Press, Lexington, KY.

Thompson, P.B. (2014) "Agricultural Ethics," in Thompson, P.B. and Kaplan, D.M. eds., *Encyclopedia of Food and Agricultural Ethics*, Springer, Dordrecht, 54–62.

Thompson, P.B. (2016) *From Field to Fork: Field Ethics for Everyone*, Oxford University Press, Oxford.

Tlili, S. (2012) *Animals in the Qur'an*, Cambridge University Press, Cambridge.

Tucker, M.E. and Grim, J.A. (2001) "Introduction: The emerging alliance of the world religions and ecology," *Daedalus*. Available at www.amacad.org/publications/fall2001/tucker-grim.aspx (accessed June 10, 2012).

USDA (2007) "Sustainable agriculture: Definitions and terms," Special Reference Briefs Series 99–02 (September 1999; revised August 2007). Compiled by Mary V. Gold. Available at www.nal.usda.gov/afsic/pubs/terms/srb9902.shtml (accessed February 6, 2014).

Van Wieren, G. (2013) *Restored to Earth: Christianity, Environmental Ethics, and Ecological Restoration*, Georgetown University Press, Washington, DC.

Webb, S. (2001) *Good Eating*, Grand Rapids: Brazos, Ada, MI.

Wirzba, N. (2003) *Paradise of God: Renewing Religion for an Ecological Age*, Oxford University Press, New York, NY.

Wirzba, N. (2011) *Food and Faith: A Theology of Eating*, Cambridge University Press, New York, NY.

Zeller, B.E., Dallam, M.W., Neilson, R.L., and Rubel, N.L. (eds.) (2014) *Religion, Food, and Eating in North America* with Foreword by M.L. Finch, Columbia University Press, New York, NY.

1

DOWN ON THE FARM

The historical roots of the ecological crisis – agriculture?

One of the key questions that a book on food and environmental ethics must confront at the outset is whether the very activity of agriculture is adequate for fostering a healthy and durable relationship between people and nature. Some environmental thinkers have made strong arguments in favor of this position while others have vehemently disagreed. The purpose of this chapter is to examine some of environmental thought's most compelling theories for and against agriculture as a promising activity for promoting ecologically sustainable relationships and societies. 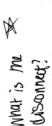 For if agricultural civilizations, including the religions that grew out of them, are in a fundamental way responsible for creating a disconnect between humans and natural world, as some environmental authors have argued, then we will need to know more precisely what it is about current agricultural practices that continue to contribute to this disconnect. Furthermore, if alternative forms of agriculture have the capacity to restore people's relationship to Earth, as this book claims, then we will need to know which practices in particular foster such connections, and how more exactly they are developed.

The chapter proceeds as follows. It begins by examining critiques of agriculture's ecologically destructive ways as represented in the work of evolutionary psychologist Paul Shepard and medieval historian Lynn White, Jr. Next, I recount several pro-agricultural environmental perspectives as exemplified in the thought of essayist Wendell Berry, physicist and environmental activist Vandana Shiva, and Christian theologian Norman Wirzba. In the end, I note how these distinct perspectives help to inform the book's overall approach, and, in addition, how they represent, to varying degrees, what I am calling restorative forms of agriculture.

Farming as an ecological disease

Among the most convincing arguments against agriculture as a model for human ecological life was developed by the late American environmentalist and evolutionary

what is the disconnect?

psychologist Paul Shepard (1925–1996). Considered the founder of the study of human ecology and a pioneer in the study of the root causes of the current ecological crisis, Shepard began developing his theory, now referred to as the "Pleistocene paradigm," in the 1950s while a doctoral student at Yale University. His first book, *Man in the Landscape: A Historic View of the Esthetics of Nature* (1967) – printed the same year as Lynn White Jr.'s now famous essay in the journal *Science*, "The Historical Roots of Our Ecologic Crisis" – was based on his graduate thesis, and is still considered Shepard's most seminal work. In a foreword to a reprinted edition of Shepard's *Man in the Landscape* (1967, 2002), radical environmentalist and founder of the social movement organization, Earth First! Dave Foreman wrote that Shepard's "books are demanding. They aren't nature fluff…Shepard is challenging to read because most people – nature lovers included – can't handle the truth," that is, "that our species is fundamentally part of the Pleistocene" and that "our emperor (agriculture-based civilization) [wears] no clothes" (Foreman, foreword to Shepard, 1967, 2002, x). Shepard's subsequent books, most notably, *The Tender Carnivore and the Sacred Game* (1973, 1998a) and *Coming Home to the Pleistocene* (1998b), detail his theory that we are essentially "beings of the Pleistocene," with brains, bodies, and consciousness that developed evolutionarily and historically through our encounters as hunter–gatherers with the natural world.

Shepard's Pleistocene theory develops along the following lines. Ninety-nine percent of human history has been spent living in the natural, mostly outdoor, environment; agriculture, as a mode of producing food, was developed relatively recent in the human social record. The earliest estimates of agriculture's beginnings, as the prominent geographer Carl Sauer suggested, trace to approximately 9,000 BCE, where at least two groups of farmers in the Near East, the Natufian and the Karim Shahirian were found buried with what is believed to be the bones of domestic sheep, goats, and two types of grains. Yet the human genome, notes Shepard, was solidified some 100,000, that is 91,000 years before the dawn of agriculture. If we further consider the emergence of organized agricultural civilizations, namely those that arose in the great Mesopotamia river valleys around 3,000 BCE, the mode of hunter–gatherer characterized 97,000 out of 100,000 years of our stabilized genetic history. If we widen that to include the whole of human evolutionary history, it represents approximately 5,000 years of agriculture to 2 million years of hunting and gathering.

Shepard refers to the agricultural era of human history as "ten thousand years of crisis" (1973, 1998a, 2). Farming, he writes in no uncertain terms, is "an ecological disease" (33).

> The disaster facing us now is a continuation of an earth trauma that began about ten thousand years ago [with the advent of agriculture]. There was a shift to a new way of life at that time, a shift still taking place across the earth, a civilizing, progressive commitment to conflict with the natural world and with ourselves.
>
> *(34)*

The notion that agriculture may foster respect for the soil is a myth that does not stand careful examination, Shepard argues, citing United States soil scientist Walter Lowdermilk's 1930s research study on the tragic state of soil's degradation wrought worldwide by all of the major agricultural civilizations. Shepard concludes that, even as such ancient agricultural technologies were relatively modest compared to today, what we share with them is a "world view generated by monocultures":

> However noble the spirit and grand the human aspirations since the earliest Egyptian dynasties may be…Its vision of a man-centered universe and impoverished ecology bedecked as destiny is a heritage too uncritically accepted…perhaps mankind has unwittingly embraced a diseased era as the model of human life.
>
> *(25)*

Shepard takes it a step further: "Peasant existence is the dullest life man ever lived," he posits (242). "The idyll of agrarian life has no basis in reality, yet how tenacious is the illusion that there is something gracious about a life of manure-shoveling, sluice-reaming, and goat-tending" (30).

The big question for Shepard is not how agricultural domestication of animals and plants engendered the human domination of land, but, in a deeper sense, how the human heart and consciousness were altered through the demise of cynegetic (hunting and its culture) life. Even today, Shepard contends, the central features of human life remain indebted to their cynegetic past, which continues to hold the clues for healthy human functioning. "If man's environmental crisis signifies a crippled state of consciousness as much as it does damaged habitat," writes Shepard, "then that is perhaps where we should begin. The secret lies in the darkness of the human cerebrum." "To see it we must turn our eyes toward the sidelong glimmer of a distant paradise that seems light-years away." (xxix)

This does not mean for Shepard that we backtrack "through the barnyard" to attempt to return to our hunter-gathering days and way of life. Modern humans, Shepard admits, cannot go back to their primitive state in practical or symbolic terms. But what we can do, Shepard suggests, is recognize that we really never left our cynegetic past: "Our home is the earth, our time the Pleistocene Ice Ages. The past is the formula for our being. Cynegetic man is us" (260). The choice before us is clear, argues Shepard: industrial agriculture or techno-cynegetics. The new cynegetics, Shepard proposes, "is not a vision of a lost paradise; it is inevitable, a necessity if we are to survive at all" (278).

For Shepard, the problem is one of land use and how human settlements have been organized. Following the work of Greek urban planner Constantinos A. Doxiadis and Italian planner Paolo Soleri, Shepard proposes that cities have populations of approximately 50,000, with no more than a ten-minute walk to city centers. This way they could be constructed on the perimeters of continents, like ribbons, with the interior freed for the evolution of ecological systems and cynegetic cultural use. Buildings would be built high above and deep below ground so to minimize land use for architecture. Such is not the sketch of a utopia, according to Shepard. Rather, it presents an opportunity to "confront the division between man and the rest of nature, between ourselves as animals and as humans, not by the destruction of nature or by a return to some dream of the past, but by creating a new civilization" (278).

Shepard states that his vision for cynegetic civilization does not require abandoning modern technologies or really anything else. Quite the opposite, in the area of food, it would mean developing new, cutting-edge technologies that would in turn allow for the disbanding of gigantic industrialized land use. What we would eat and use would come largely from factories that synthesize microbial foods from preexistent sources in nature. The extraction of protein from green leaves, for instance, has been available since the 1940s as Shepard points out. Examples such as these prove that plants can be grown in mediums and spaces besides field-based agriculture.

The transition to non-land-based food sources may take a half a century, Shepard accepts, but it could help free a large portion of the Earth from current destructive use. Domestic animals could also be freed in this new way of life, save for their use for psychotherapeutic or religious purposes, according to Shepard. The education of children is among the most important tasks in Shepard's ecological society. Every child under ten would have three basic ecological needs met: she would have a complex play space shared with companions, a diverse experience of nonhuman forms whose names would be learned, and progressively strenuous excursions into the wild world. It may be impossible for modern adults to develop deep, spiritual relationships to and perception of the natural world, Shepard believes, but they can help their children and their children's children develop such a worldview.

Shepard's closed-shut critique of agriculture – and not just modern large-scale industrial agriculture but even early subsistence and small-scale agriculture of the family farm type – and the techno-cynegetic alternative it necessitates hints at some of the hi- and low-tech alternatives being proposed by those in the new food and food justice movements, including, for instance, new ventures in indoor vertical farming and urban hunting and foraging. Even as Shepard's model may not present a viable option for the scale of an agricultural system that will be required to feed an expanding global population, it nevertheless provides a useful theory for contemplating the root causes of the current environmental crisis. For while agricultural civilization may be Shepard's culprit, the deeper, underlying problem he spotlights is the type of nature-alienated consciousness that characterizes modern human beings. The question is whether the practice of agriculture really is the activity that has shaped such alienated consciousness or whether there are other ideas, beliefs, and practices that are more fundamentally to blame.

Anthropocentric Christianity and mechanized agriculture

In 1966, UCLA historian Lynn White, Jr. famously presented a lecture at the Association of the American Academy of Science meeting titled "The Historic Roots of our Ecologic Crisis," which was published in the journal *Science* a year later.[1] Although White discussed the role of technological innovations, it was his hypothesis about the role of religion in environmental decline that created a decades-long furor. He acknowledged at the article's outset how little we know about the types of cultural inputs that have historically created negative environmental conditions. Still, White argued that it was the scientific technological innovations developed in medieval Europe, wedded with a "Judeo–Christian" worldview that had been especially pernicious in the Western exploitation of nature. According to White, the

Christian interpretation of the dominion texts in the Hebrew bible (Genesis 1:26), as well as its transcendent view of God and otherworldly view of salvation, led to an instrumental, anthropocentric, and disenchanted view of the natural world. The disenchantment could be traced to the wider monotheistic antipathy toward pagan animism, which led Christians to eradicate sacred groves as "idolatrous because they assume spirit in nature" (White 1967, 1206). This view, White averred, fit well with the mechanized, static understanding of nature, with "man" as its superior and active conqueror, which developed through the Middle Ages and sixteenth and seventeenth century scientific revolution and Protestant Reformation in Europe. It was this nexus of Western science and technology motivated by a Christian anthropocentric worldview that led to the current environmental crisis, and these ideas, White argued, continue to influence environment-related attitudes and behaviors, even in the increasingly secular world.

Different from Shepard, it was White's hypothesis about the role of religion, especially Christianity, and by association the other biblical faiths, in instantiating ecological destruction that gained the most attention. Most of this scholarship has focused on White's interpretation of the Genesis texts and Christian theology's influence on the development of destructive environmental worldviews. Few scholars, however, have spent much time analyzing the other key variable in White's thesis: the historical shift in tillage methods. As White notes, the scratch plow pulled by two oxen was until the middle part of the seventh century the main implement used for plowing fields in the Near East and Mediterranean region. Since soil in these semi-arid regions was relatively light, the land's surface could be sufficiently agitated for planting by pulling a plow in a back and forth pattern on top of fields, which tended to be square in size. The soil in northern Europe, however, was wet and heavy, yielding the scratch-cross plow method ineffective for digging into and turning the dirt. Thus, by the latter part of the seventh century, some northern European peasants began to use a different type of plow, which cut into the dirt with a vertical knife, sliced under the sod with a horizontal share, and then turned it over with a moldboard.

Given the amount of friction this new plow produced, eight oxen, rather than two, were required to pull it. Yet peasants, who typically farmed one field per family unit, did not own eight oxen, which meant resources needed to be pooled in order to develop teams of oxen. The shape of fields also changed to accommodate the new tillage method since the knife cutting plow no longer required crisscrossing a field with a horse team of eight, which was difficult to turn. Now it made more sense for fields to be long and narrow, rather than square. Families were thus portioned a strip of plowed land according to the amount of resources (land and oxen) they contributed to the pool. This meant, White concluded, that "distribution of land was based no longer on the needs of a family but, rather, on the capacity of a power machine to till the earth. Man's relation to the soil was profoundly changed. Formerly man had been part of nature; now he was the exploiter of nature" (1967, 1205).

For White, then, it was not agricultural activity itself that was to blame for the current environmental crisis, rather an anthropocentric religious worldview that shaped cultural shifts in how human beings understood themselves in relation to the natural world. Furthermore, White believed that even though increasing numbers in the West were secular, Western society's basic values continued to be shaped by an anthropocentric form of Christianity, which would contribute to "a worsening ecologic crisis" unless the "Christian axiom that nature has no reason for existence save to serve man" was rejected (1207). As an alternative to an environmentally destructive type of Christian anthropocentrism, White considered Zen Buddhism as a tradition that had some affinity with positive nature–spirituality, though, in the end, he viewed it as too foreign to Western society to significantly change it. Instead, White suggested Saint Francis of Assisi as a paradigmatic model for promoting a healthier human/nature relationship as Francis "tried to depose man from his monarchy over creation and set up a democracy of all God's creatures" (1207). Further, Francis' "view of nature and of man rested on a unique sort of pan-psychism of all things animate and inanimate, designed for the glorification of their transcendent Creator" (1207). White famously concluded his article in *Science* with the following admonishment: "We must rethink and refeel our nature and destiny. The profoundly religious, but heretical, sense of the primitive Franciscans for the spiritual autonomy of all parts of nature may point a direction. I propose Francis as a patron saint for ecologists." A few years later, White made even clearer what sort of religious prescription he had in mind, indicating that what was needed was a felt sense of belonging to nature and a belief in the agency and intrinsic value of all life. Speaking of Western peoples, he wrote, "Man-nature dualism is deep-rooted in us" and "until it is eradicated not only from our minds but also from our emotions, we shall doubtless be unable to make fundamental changes in our attitudes and actions affecting ecology. The religious problem is to find a viable equivalent to animism" (1972, 62).

Whether a more nature-sensitive tillage method would be induced by such an animistic spirituality, White did not hypothesize. Still, such a prospect generates several questions relevant for our inquiry. For example: What more precisely would a spiritually animistic-based type of farming look like? We have numerous accounts of the characteristics that mark different types of animistic religiosity, from indigenous to pagan to Abrahamic forms, though what about their agricultural upshots?[2] And if we do in fact have examples of this type of agriculture, what are its defining features? These are among the questions we will return to as chapters unfold. For now, we examine another type of argument against current forms of agriculture, one that faults neither religion nor agriculture per se, but rather the specific form of agriculture developed by Western industrial, capitalist culture.

Bad farming, good farming

Chief among those writers that have issued critiques of Western industrial agriculture for its global capitalist orientation are American essayist Wendell Berry and Indian physicist Vandana Shiva. As we saw in this book's introduction, Berry and Shiva have over the past four decades written passionate pleas against the neoliberal economic policies that have shaped Western agricultural development (or, maldevelopment, in Shiva's terms) for their devastating impacts on traditional farming systems, land health, and biodiversity. Instead, they have argued for the defense of what Berry has called "good farming," or, in other words, "farming as defined by agrarianism as opposed to farming as defined by industrialism: farming as the proper use and care of an immeasurable gift" (2003, 24).

Industrial farming is problematic on several accounts according to Berry and Shiva. First, industrialism is based on an inadequate model for understanding what is going on in the world and in life. "The way of industrialism is the way of the machine," writes Berry. He continues:

> To the industrial mind, a machine is not merely an instrument for doing work or amusing ourselves or making war; it is an explanation of the world and of life. The machine's entirely comprehensible articulation of parts defines the acceptable meanings of our experience, and it prescribes the kinds of meanings the industrial scientists and scholars expect to discover. These meanings have to do with nomenclature, classification, and rather short lineages of causation. Because industrialism cannot understand living things except as machines, and can grant them no value that is not utilitarian, it conceives of farming and forestry as forms of mining; it cannot use the land without abusing it.
>
> *(Berry 2003, 24)*

Shiva emphasizes the militaristic orientation of industrial agriculture, calling it a "war against ecosystems" (2003, 122). Military–industrial agriculture, she writes, "is based on the instruments of war and the logic of war, and it has warlike consequences" (122). Take for example the type and names of chemicals used in industrial agriculture. They are the same chemicals that were originally used for chemical warfare, with names that reflect their military orientation: "Machete," "Pentagon," "Prowl," "Avenge," as Shiva observes, are herbicides manufactured by Monsanto and their affiliate American Home Products (123). Shiva argues that such militaristic forms of corporate agriculture reflect the same patriarchal, aggressive, and competitive mentality that undergirded the Green Revolution. Monocultures and monopolies, writes Shiva, "symbolize a masculinization of agriculture" which is destroying both "the economic basis of survival for the poorest women in the rural areas of the Third World" and the genetic diversity of traditional farming systems (122). Large-scale monoculture crops of wheat and rice, which have a narrow genetic base, replaced the mixture of native diverse crops such as oilseeds, millets, and legumes, which contain a high genetic variability. This meant the irreversible loss of species diversity and ecosystem resilience, and the diminishment of certain cultural values. Shiva writes that "as diversity gave way to monocultures, cultures of peace and sharing gave way to cultures of violence. It was not peace but war that was the legacy of the Green Revolution" (125).

The global market economy that military-industrial agriculture prescribes is "placeless and displacing," Berry adds (2003, 24). It applies "its methods and technologies indiscriminately in the American East and the American West, in the United States and India" (24). For this reason, Shiva argues that she recognizes the same patterns Berry writes about in *The Unsettling of America* unfolding in her native India, with the globalization of industrial agriculture replicating an economy of colonialism. As with the colonialist mentality, industrial agriculture "destroys locally adapted agrarian economies everywhere it goes simply because it is too ignorant not to do so," states Berry (25). The industrial solution, Berry writes "is to bring Big Ideas, Big Money, and Big Technology into small rural communities, economies, and ecosystems—the brought-in industry and the experts being invariably alien to and contemptuous of the places to which they are brought in" (26).

Conversely, agrarian agriculture, or, "good farming," begins with the idea that there are certain givens in Earthly life that humans did not create and are born into. Knowledge of agriculture is a birthright, a given, for Berry and Shiva, along with land, plants, animals, and weather. Berry puts it in religious terms: "Agrarians understand themselves as the users and caretakers of some things they did not make, and of some things that they cannot make;" "to agrarianism farming is the proper use and care of an immeasurable gift" (26). Citing the biblical idea of creation as a gift from God as interpretation of agrarian values such as these, Berry also quotes Gerard Manley Hopkins famous poem, "God's Grandeur": "The world is charged with the grandeur of God" (as cited in Berry 2003, 26).

Berry's and Shiva's arguments against industrial agriculture resonate with those working in the food and faith movement. For as we shall see as this book's chapters unfold, many of these groups and individuals cite agrarian ideals related to community life, self-sufficiency, and citizenship as a basis for their work. Some environmental justice and feminist philosophers have critiqued agrarian proposals for their anti-urban and overly romantic bias which portrays at times a nostalgic and unattainable desire for a past way of life in which people lived more harmoniously, fruitfully, and happily with land.[3] Further, agrarian proposals have been accused of neglecting the issue of difference both between human and nonhuman and between diverse biological entities, as well as within the human community.

One of the interesting aspects of the agrarian oriented narratives put forward by some groups working in the food and faith movement, as we shall see, is the way in which they at times emphasize notions both of community and difference, harmony and justice. This raises additional questions for contemporary agrarian theory in terms of how it may be reconfigured in light of hands-on agricultural and food-based experiences. Further, Berry's and Shiva's appeals to religious thought generate additional questions about how agrarian farming may elucidate interpretations of certain nature-based spiritual approaches and experiences. With this in mind, I turn to a final critique of industrial agriculture, one that explicitly considers agrarian philosophy and religious narrative.

Eating in exile

Similar to White's argument, Christian theologian Norman Wirzba views the current ecological crisis as fundamentally a spiritual crisis. Different from White, however, Wirzba emphasizes what he views as beneficial, agrarian resonant narratives in Hebrew and Christian scriptures. In this way Wirzba's approach echoes Shiva's with her retrieval of sacred texts for contemplating contemporary agricultural and ecological problems and people's relationship to the Earth. For Wirzba, today's eco-logical (and economic and physiological) ills related to the global food system are symptoms of a Western cultural condition of exile, where humans have become alienated from the natural world and from God, a condition that Christians call sin. On this, Wirzba writes:

> To be in exile does not simply mean that we are in the wrong place – a problem of location and logistics. It also means that the ways and manners of our being anywhere do not exhibit a harmonious fit – a problem of moral and spiritual discernment…to be in exile marks an inability to live peaceably, sustainable, and joyfully in one's place. Not knowing or loving where we are and who we are with, we don't know how to live in ways that foster mutual flourishing and delight. More specifically we don't know how through our eating to live sympathetically into the memberships that make creation a life-giving home.
>
> *(2011, 72)*

The problems associated with the current food crisis may, in other words, be caused by the industrial policies of governmental and corporate backed agriculture, the Green Revolution, and a hyper-growth driven global free-market economy, according to Wirzba. But at the deepest level, Wirzba suggests, they are rooted in an inability to recognize our true place and role as human citizens in the community of creation. "In our often thoughtless and aggressive hoarding of the gifts of God," states Wirzba, "we demonstrate again and again the anxiety of membership" (72). The degradation of the soil and water, the depletion of fisheries and forests, the loss of genetic diversity and ecosystem integrity, all of these, Wirzba suggests reflect an adversarial relationship to the rest of creation.

Wirzba proposes that the human alienation from nature, God, and even from one's own body, is best narrated for Christians in terms of the Genesis account of the fall of Adam and Eve in the garden of Eden. The first biblical transgression, Wirzba recounts, is an eating transgression. Adam and Eve are exiled from the gar-den because they *eat* the fruit from the forbidden tree. "How are we to understand this refusal to eat and live appropriately in the garden?" Wirzba wonders. "Why do people rebel against the limits, demands, and joy that gardens embody?" (25).

Wirzba's response focuses on the primordial fall as a paradigmatic example of humanity's refusal to recognize the limits of creaturely finitude and the neces-sity of relationships. The first human transgression represents the lack of conscious awareness of appropriate boundaries among the created, including human creatures, and God as creator. Judgments about what constitutes good and evil such as those spelled out in the creation stories represent one of the oldest forms of boundary-making. According to Wirzba: "To transgress a boundary is to do evil. To observe a boundary is to do what is right. To have no bounds is to be a god. Because we are

God's creatures we are clearly finite and in need of help of others, which means that we live within and in terms of memberships of nurture, memberships that make life possible but also entail certain responsibilities on our part to serve and protect the garden (Genesis 2:15)" (25). Denial of membership and responsibility in the garden of life, therefore, represents a transgression of boundaries, creating the false dream that humans can transcend their creaturely needs and in effect become a supernatural god without need of earthly goods. On this reading, Adam and Eve's exile from the garden is a symbolic representation of what happens when humans are unwilling to embrace the limits of their created need for and dependence on others.

Still, the act of eating is inherently paradoxical, according to Wirzba. On the one hand, it provides the context for the human fall into sin; on the other hand, it provides a context for understanding and practicing and enjoying our lives as inter-related members of creation. Wirzba quotes Dietrich Bonhoeffer's interpretation of the fall to explain what he considers the unavoidable human condition of the "anxiety of membership." For Bonhoeffer "The Fall…is revolt…it is the destruction of creatureliness. It is defection, it is the fall from being held in creatureliness…it is not simply a moral lapse but the destruction of creation by the creature." (as cited in Wirzba 2011, 76–77). A Christian experiences anxiety of membership, according to Wirzba, when he runs from the responsibility and the gift that he is both needed by others and that he needs them; ultimately, it is a rejection of creaturely interdependence as God intended. Modern industrial forms of eating violate the spiritual capacity to recognize and live into such forms of interdependent relationships with other people, organisms, and the land community. They are, for Wirzba, a sin, a violation of God and creation and a Christian's deepest self.[4] Like Berry and Shiva, a more agrarian, community-based form of agriculture and eating has the capacity to provide a promising counterweight to such a spiritually fraught state of existence. In the next and final section, we explore what this might look like.

From industrial to restorative agriculture

The four perspectives on agriculture just described will each contribute, to varying degrees and in various ways, to the argument that is developed in the pages that follow. Following Shepard's lead, I consider how certain types of agricultural practices and the landscapes necessary to support them may induce or inhibit the development of an ecological consciousness, including its spiritual and moral dimensions. White's argument against Christian anthropocentrism in particular and Abrahamic faiths in general will need to be addressed, despite its well-wornness, for one will want to know how biblical and theological interpretations of nature, humanity, and the divine are, or are not, being reconfigured where religious communities and individuals are participating in ethical food actions. Agrarian accounts such as Berry's have repeatedly been critiqued for their utopian and romantic biases and neglect to consider matters of justice, difference, and multiplicity, yet emerging varieties of faith-based agrarian efforts, including those with environmental justice objectives such as Shiva's, call such criticisms into question and necessitate further evaluation. Wirzba's approach provides a symbolic interpretation of agriculture and eating that will help us think about farming as a form of spiritual practice, though in this book's case cross-religious perspectives will need to be considered more than his account allows.

Even as the above accounts are varied and diverse, what they share is a critique of and alternative vision to the current system of industrial agriculture and the cultural values that undergird it. While they present no single model or interpretation of alternative agriculture, they do nevertheless represent various themes of what I am calling "restorative agriculture." Restorative agriculture, recall, represents food and farming work that is good for the Earth and good for the human soul. It serves to promote the flourishing of natural processes and systems while connecting people to particular landed places in ways that enliven the human spirit and communities. How restorative agriculture and its values are enacted and interpreted will of course vary from community to community and culture to culture. Still, as we shall see in the pages that unfold, there are common threads in this narrative, including how agriculture's most basic element is understood. Thus, we begin in the next chapter literally from the ground up – with the soil.

Notes

1 For more on the scholarly impact of White's essay and a review of the social scientific literature that has since tested it, see the multi-year study by Bron Taylor, Bernard Zaleha, and myself, published in the following articles: Bron Raymond Taylor (2016), "The Greening of Religion Hypothesis (Part One): From Lynn White, Jr. claims that religions can promote environmentally destructive attitudes and behaviors to assertions they are becoming environmentally friendly" (2006a); Bron Raymond Taylor, Gretel Van Wieren, and Bernard Daly Zaleha, "The Greening of Religion Hypothesis (Part Two): Assessing the Data from Lynn White, Jr., to Pope Francis" (2006b); Bron Raymond Taylor, Gretel Van Wieren, and Bernard Daly Zaleha, "Lynn White Jr. and the greening-of-religion hypothesis" (2006c). I am indebted to these articles for the discussion of White here.
2 See, for example, Bron Taylor's *Dark Green Religion: Nature Spirituality and the Planetary Future* (Berkeley, CA: University of California Press, 2010).
3 See for example the work of Iris Marion Young, including *Justice and the Politics of Difference* (1990).
4 Traditional accounts of the doctrine of sin suggest that human pride lies at its root. Feminist theologians and ethicists have questioned this idea, instead arguing that it is pride-*lessness*, based on an overemphasis on self-sacrificial behavior that better characterizes the experiences of women in particular. According to this view, sin stems not from a lack of awareness of one's dependence on and relationship with others, but rather from an excessive sense of such dependence and relationality. Extending this critique to environmental concerns, narratives that emphasize the idea that environmental problems stem from a transgression of human freedom and limits will require critical retrieval and reinterpretation. For a feminist critique of pride as the root sin, see the classic essay by Valerie Saiving Goldstein, "The Human Situation: A Feminine View," *The Journal of Religion*, 40(2), 100–12.

References

Berry, W. (2003) "The agrarian standard," in N. Wirzba (ed.), *The Essential Agrarian Reader: The Future of Culture, Community, and the Land*, University of Kentucky Press, Lexington, KY, 23–33.

Foreman, D. (2002) Foreword to P. Shepard, *Man in the Landscape: A Historic View of the Esthetics of Nature*, University of Georgia Press, Athens (original printing, 1967), Knopf, New York, NY.

Shepard, P. (1973, 1998a) *The Tender Carnivore and the Sacred Game*, Scribner, New York, NY.

Shepard, P. (1998b) *Coming Home to the Pleistocene*, Island Press, Washington, DC.

Shiva, V. (2003) "The war against farmers and the land," in N. Wirzba (ed.), *The Essential Agrarian Reader: The Future of Culture, Community, and the Land*, University of Kentucky Press, Lexington, KY, 121–139.

Taylor, B.R. (2016) "The greening of religion hypothesis (part one): From Lynn White, Jr. claims that religions can promote environmentally destructive attitudes and behaviors to assertions they are becoming environmentally friendly," *Journal for the Study of Religion, Nature and Culture* (10)3, 268–305.

Taylor, B.R., Van Wieren, G., Zaleha, B.D. (2016a) "The greening of religion hypothesis (part two): Assessing the data from Lynn White, Jr., to Pope Francis," *Journal for the Study of Religion, Nature and Culture* 10(3), 306–78.

Taylor, B.R., Van Wieren, G., Zaleha, B.D. (2016b) "Lynn White Jr. and the greening-of-religion hypothesis," *Conservation Biology* 30(5), 1000–1009.

White Jr., L. (1967) "The historic roots of our ecologic crisis," *Science* 155, 1203–7.

White Jr., L. (1973) "Continuing the conversation" in I. G. Barbour, *Western Man and Environmental Ethics*, Addison-Wesley, Menlo Park, CA, 55–64.

Wirzba, N. (2011) *Food and Faith: A Theology of Eating*, Cambridge University Press, Cambridge.

Young, I.M. (1990) *Justice and the Politics of Difference*, Princeton University Press, Princeton, NJ.

2
SOIL
Sacred and profaned

The soil, too—let others pen-and-ink the sea, the air, (as I sometimes try)—but now I feel to choose the common soil for theme—naught else. The brown soil here, just between winter-close and opening spring and vegetation—the rain-shower at night, and the fresh smell next morning—the red worms wriggling out of the ground—the dead leaves, the incipient grass, and the latent life underneath—the effort to start something—already in shelter'd spots some little flowers—the distant emerald show of winter wheat and the rye-fields—the yet naked trees, with clear interstices, giving prospects hidden in summer—the tough fallow and the plow-team, and the stout boy whistling to his horses for encouragement—and there the dark fat earth in long slanting stripes upturn'd.

(Walt Whitman's "The Common Earth, The Soil")

Since ancient times, cultures and religions worldwide have viewed soil in sacred terms. In Indian thought, for example, soil is viewed as the sacred Mother and source of all fertility, the cradle of civilization and daily life.[1] In the Hebrew bible, God is understood to have scooped up dirt (*adamah*) and breathed in life. From this divine infused *adamah* emerged *adam*, the primordial human being. In fact, "humanity (*adam*) is what it is, *is* at all" in Jewish and Christian thought "because of its relation to soil (*adamah*) and the life God makes possible through it" (Wirzba 2011, 39). Islam views the whole of nature, including the most minute and intricate elements, as reflections of the divine creator, created order, and balance of the universe. As Islamic environmental ethicist, Ibrahim Özdemir notes: "The seven heavens and the earth, and all beings therein, declare His glory: there is not a thing but celebrates His praise (Qur'an 17:44)" (2003, 16).

Yet modern agriculture has not taken such views about soil's sacred quality to heart. This is not to say, as Paul Thompson suggests, that modern agriculture should be deified. Rather, Western society's demystification of agriculture "errs when it conceives of nature as lifeless, or of humanity as essentially separate from the production of food" (1995, 19). Industrial cultures have waged war against the soil, states *Dirt!*, a 2009 documentary based on New York City arborist William Bryant Logan's acclaimed 1995 book with the same title. Soil, the film narrates, has become just "stupid dirt." But how, we might ask, did this happen? How did dirt go from being viewed as the sacred, holy ground of life to just stupid, valueless matter to be manipulated and pushed around?

Defining dirt

In *Dirt*, Logan begins with a confession:

> The truth is that we don't know the first thing about dirt. We don't even know where it comes from. All we can say is that it doesn't come from here. Our own sun is too young and cool to manufacture any element heavier than helium. Helium is number two on the periodic table, leaving some ninety elements on earth that were not even made in our solar system. Uranium and plutonium, the heaviest elements that occur in nature, can be forged only in an exploding star, a supernova. 'We are all stardust,' says a friend of mine. He understates the case. In fact, *everything* is stardust."
>
> *(1995, 7)*

Some two centuries prior to Bryant's writing, Boston-born philosopher of nature Ralph Waldo Emerson made a similar observation about the common makeup of earthly matter.

> The whole code of [Nature's] laws may be written on the thumbnail, or the signet of a ring. The whirling bubble on the surface of a brook, admits us to the secret of the mechanics of the sky. Every shell on the beach is a key to it. A little water made to rotate in a cup explains the formation of the simpler shells; the addition of matter from year to year, arrives at last at the most complex form; and yet so poor is nature with all her craft, that, from the beginning to the end of the universe, she has but one stuff, – but one stuff with its two ends, to serve up all her dream-like variety. Compound it how she will, star, sand, fire, water, tree, man, it is still one stuff, and betrays the same properties.
>
> *(1884, 389)*

But can this actually be true? Is everything really stardust? Are we truly the same stuff as stars, sand, and dirt?

Yes and no. On the one hand, we know from elementary school life science that matter is matter is matter; on the other hand, not all matter is created equally. Soil, for example, is not the same as dirt, as noted in one primer on soil, *Know Soil Know Life*, published by the Soil Science Society of America (SSSA). "Dirt is the stuff under your fingernails; it is what you sweep up off the floor; it is unwanted and unnecessary. Soil, on the other hand, is essential for life," "a living, dynamic resource at the surface of the earth" (Lindbo, Kozlowski, Robinson, 2012, 6). The primer goes onto define soil as "a natural, three-dimensional body at the Earth's surface. It is capable of supporting plants and has properties resulting from the effects of climate and living matter acting on earthy parent material, as conditioned by relief and by the passage of time" (6).

Four fundamental components make up every type of soil: minerals, organic matter (living and dead), water, and air. *Know Soil Know Life* calls these the "modern view of the alchemists' four elements that we cannot live without" (6). Water and air represent soil's pore space, minerals and organic matter, its solid phase. If one were to pick up a handful of soil, it would typically contain 50 percent pore space and 50 percent solid phase, with 45–50 percent minerals, and 0–5 percent organic matter. It would also contain more organisms than there are human beings living on Earth.

Soil types are incredibly varied and diverse. One only needs to think of the major terrestrial biomes — savanna and temperate rainforests, boreal and temperate forests, arctic and alpine tundra, deserts, shrublands, and wetlands — to begin to realize the extent of a particular soil type's uniqueness. Soils have different colors, textures, consistencies, and structures, with different relations between sand, silt, and clay. Soil can be loose, firm, friable (slight finger force — like rich crumbly cake), or rigid (light blows; hit the sample with a hammer), and many other consistencies in between. It can be nonsticky or very sticky; nonplastic or very plastic in terms of whether it can be rolled into a "wire" (26).

Still, soil scientist, Daniel Hillel cautions against the attempt to reach a precise definition of soil, "for what we commonly call soil is anything but a homogeneous entity" (Hillel 1991, 24). Soil is in fact elusive, he observes, "an exceedingly variable body with a wide range of attributes" (24). Hillel concludes that perhaps the best we can do is to offer a basic definition of soil as "the fragmented outer layer of the earth's terrestrial surface in which the living roots of plants can obtain anchorage and sustenance, alongside a thriving biotic community of microscopic and macroscopic organisms" (24). Writing a half of a century earlier, founder of the modern-day conservation movement Aldo Leopold famously wrote about soil's integral role in the "revolving fund of life." "Land is not merely soil," he famously wrote in "The Land Ethic," rather "it is a fountain of energy flowing through a circuit of soils, plants, and animals" (Leopold 1949,1987, 253).

Perhaps most relevant to our inquiry is the fact soil is vernacular, which is to say that it has its own particular context, cultural interfaces, and character that has been shaped over millennia and in conjunction with literally millions of inorganic and organic beings. In his classic 1941 volume, *The Soils That Support Us*, soil scientist Charles Kellogg puts it thus:

> Each soil has had its own history. Like a river, a mountain, a forest, or any
> natural thing, its present condition is due to the influences of many things

and events of the past. Nature has endowed the earth with glorious wonders and vast resources that man may use for his own ends. Regardless of our tastes or our way of living, there are none that present more variations to tax our imagination than the soil, and certainly none so important to our ancestors, to ourselves, and to our children.

(Kellogg 1941, vii)

In a similar vein, Wendell Berry writes, "The soil is the great connector of lives, the source and destination of all. It is the healer and restorer and resurrector, by which disease passes into health, age into youth, death into life…It is impossible to contemplate the life of the soil for very long without seeing it as analogous to the life of the spirit" (Berry 1977, 86). Thompson calls it "the spirit of the soil" as the title of his 1995 volume suggests. "Agriculture is, in short, a natural activity, properly emergent within many of the ecosystems in which the human species is found," writes Thompson (Thompson 1995, 19). "To speak this way is to take the earth, the soils, the waters as living, if not animated, and to understand this life is to seek, in some sense the spirit of the soil" (19).

Desecrated soil

In the late 1930s, Chief of Research of the Soil Conservation Service of the U.S. federal government Walter C. Lowdermilk undertook a transglobal research project to study the history of land use and soil health among the world's great civilization. Over the course of fifteen months, Lowdermilk traveled over 30,000 miles by plane, train, automobile, boat, and foot to examine soil erosion, soil and water conservation, and flood control regimes in Egypt, Algeria, Tunisia, Libya, Trans-Jordan, Palestine, Lebanon, Syria, Iraq, Italy, France, Holland, Scotland, and England. Prior to these travels he had made five research trips to the interior of northern China.

Toward the end of his travels, Lowdermilk gave a radio address in Jerusalem, which formed the basis of his 1940 article, "The Eleventh Commandment" that appeared in the journal *American Forests*. The ten commandments delivered by Moses, Lowdermilk proposed, were in need of an additional commandment as a way "to regulate man's relation and responsibility to Mother Earth, whose cultivation and production must nourish all generations" (Lowdermilk 1940, 12). Lowdermilk further postulated:

> If Moses had anticipated what we have seen in north China, Korea, north Africa, Asia Minor, Mesopotamia and our own United States; namely, the wastage of land due to man's practices of suicidal agriculture and the resulting man-made deserts and ruined civilizations, if he had foreseen the impoverishment, revolutions, wars, migrations, and social decadence of billions of peoples through thousands of years and the oncoming desolation of their lands, he doubtless would have been inspired to deliver an "Eleventh" Commandment

to complete the trinity of man's responsibilities – to his Creator, to his fellow men, and to Mother Earth.

(12)

Lowdermilk's essay catalogued what he characterized as the sins of civilization against the land. It is worth quoting at length for his passionate plea, rare I would surmise among today's federal conservation agents, to recognize the tragedy of soil degradation worldwide. "Mesopotamia [is] literally covered with miniature mountain ranges of silt, some ten, twenty and up to fifty feet in height, piled beside the ancient irrigation ditches," he wrote (13). "The staggering soil wastage of North China is unbelievable...hundreds of millions of acres have been seriously reduced from productivity to barren slopes and labyrinths of gullies" (13). "The exploitation of great areas, whether in America, Africa, Australia, or elsewhere, where farmers and stockmen have cleared and grazed new lands at a rate hitherto unknown, tell the same story [of]...the transformation of fertile plains from luxuriant vegetation, into barren windswept desert-like lands, periodically whirling blizzards of fine soils to parts unknown, and leaving behind sandy hummock" (14). By the end of Lowdermilk's cross-continental journey he concluded that he was "deeply moved by the futility, wastefulness and ineffable sadness of man's effort to adjust himself to the land. Everywhere in the ancient home of mankind one sees decadence, ruins, fragments of a greater past. It is an arresting tragedy" (15).

Lowdermilk was writing in the decade following the American Dustbowl, considered the greatest human induced ecological disaster in United States history. Since then we have learned a great deal about what is necessary for the conservation and restoration of soil health. Yet the tragedy of soil's demise in the hands of agriculture continues, arguably in even more pernicious forms and decidedly on a much larger scale. Soil worldwide is being eroded ten to forty times faster than it is being replenished.[2] As a result, 30 percent of the Earth's arable land is now unproductive. Of the world's land that is used for crops, nearly 40 percent has reduced nutrient and water availability due to soil degradation, with one-third of this land abandoned because of degradation and erosion.

The types and causes of soil erosion differ globally by region. According to one Food and Agriculture Organization/United Nation Environment Programme (FAO/UNEP) report, in over 50 percent of the cases, water erosion degrades the soil. In nearly 30 percent of the cases it is wind erosion that leads to soil degradation. Chemical and physical degradations are responsible for another 16 percent of soil's depletion. Over 60 percent of the time such degradation is caused by agricultural activities and overgrazing of livestock, a topic we take up in Chapter 4. Deforestation, which often occurs because of the expansion of land use for agricultural purposes, is responsible for 30 percent of soil erosion and degradation.[3]

Where it was once believed that soil was invincible, an infinitely renewable resource that continually replenished itself through the cycling of nutrients and decaying matter, we now know differently. Soil scientist David Pimentel notes the alarming fact that, "It takes approximately 500 years to replace 25 millimeters

(1 inch) of topsoil lost to erosion. The minimal soil depth for agricultural production is 150 millimeters. From this perspective, productive fertile soil is a nonrenewable, endangered ecosystem."[4] In some cases soil can be restored by removing and replacing contaminated dirt, bioactivating micro-organisms, and planting vegetation. But depletion rates now outpace soil's capacity to replenish and renew itself, and not all types of degradation allow for soil's restoration.

The human costs of soil degradation are numerous and systemic to the extent that we might best think of the degradation of humans and dirt as interlinked. As Lowdermilk pointed out, entire human civilizations have risen and fallen based on how they treat dirt. Desertification and micro-deserts caused by soil erosion coupled with climate change are undermining entire country's security, with food riots in places such as Sudan arising where soil has reached such extreme levels of degradation that there remains little to no arable land to support the most basic human food needs. Soil contamination in various locales from urban to rural increasingly disallows communities from gardening and farming safe and healthy foods.

Yet not all forms of agriculture have had such a deleterious impact on soil's health. Some models of modern agriculture *have* taken soil's sacred quality to heart. Thus, we turn in the next section to examine several thinkers in twentieth century agricultural thought who sought to combine ecological and spiritual views of soil. These historical precursors will, in turn, give us clues for understanding how contemporary faith communities construe soil's sacred quality and the spiritual and moral dimensions of food and farming work associated with it.

Spiritual dimensions of sustainable agriculture

In his "A Brief History of Sustainable Agriculture," Fred Kirschenmann (2004) observes four categories of response to the industrial agriculture that developed in mid-nineteenth century Europe and the United States. The humus farming movement first emerged with influential works such as D. Browne's *The Field Book of Manures or the American Mulch Book* (1855), Charles Darwin's *The Formation of Vegetable Mould, Through the Action of Worms, With Observations on Their Habits* (1881), and, later, Albert Howard's *An Agriculture Testament* (1943), which Kirschenmann (2004) calls the bible for humus farmers. A second wave of response developed in the early twentieth century around "complex farming systems," which included key writings such as F. H. King's *Farmers of Forty Centuries* (1911) and *Soil Management* (1914). Rudolph Steiner's *Agriculture Lectures* (1924) and his vehement critique of reductionist agricultural science fostered a third movement, which resulted in "biodynamic" agriculture. Lastly, a philosophy of "organic" agriculture appeared in the 1940s in the work of Lord Northburne (*Look to the Land*, 1940), who was the first to use the term, and also in the work of Liberty Hyde Bailey (*The Holy Earth*, 1915), Lady Eve Balfour's *The Living Soil* (1943), and Louis Bromfield's *Pleasant Valley* (1946), all of which viewed the farm as a kind of self-contained organism.

Several points could be made about the spiritual elements embedded in these more holistic accounts of agriculture, including the religious resembling titles of many of the texts. Three figures in particular jump out for their explicitly spiritual interpretations of agriculture – Rudolf Steiner (1861–1925), Liberty Hyde Bailey (1858–1954), and George Washington Carver (1860s–1953), a figure not included in Kirschenmann's (2004) list of sustainable agriculture's key progenitor's, though one who is routinely drawn upon in African–American sustainable agricultural thought.[5] Each of these figures narrates a distinctive interpretation of soil's sacred quality based on their particular cultural and religious contexts. Still, their views of soil's sacredness overlap for how they understand soil's inherent vitality and spiritual significance for fostering deep relationships between people and the natural world. Moreover, intimations of these forms of nature-based spirituality are evident among many groups working in the food and faith movement, a phenomenon we will continue to unpack in the pages to follow.

Steiner's spiritual science of agriculture

Born in the Muraköz region of the Austrian Empire (today northernmost Croatia), Steiner is best known in agricultural circles for his pioneering work in the field of biodynamic farming methods and in religion circles for his unique interpretation of theosophy, which posits that divine wisdom (Greek: divine (*theo*) wisdom (*sophy*)) is discernable through direct human experience.[6] From an early age, Steiner was aware that he had a keen spiritual sense about the world, a perception that blossomed through his explorations of the Austrian countryside and through a friendship that he developed with a village priest, despite the fact that his family was not religious. Steiner went on to gain a scholarship at the Vienna Institute of Technology where he studied a wide variety of subjects from philosophy and literature to mathematics, biology, chemistry, physics, and botany. Although he did not matriculate, Steiner was recommended by one of his teachers, Karl Julius Schröer, to become the editor of the natural science volume of a new edition of Goethe's works. Steiner was later invited to become editor of the Goethe archives in Weimer, where he worked from 1888 to 1896. He eventually wrote two books on Goethe's thought, *The Theory of Knowledge Implicit in Goethe's World-Conception* (1886) and *Goethe's Conception of the World* (1897), as well as an essay, "Goethe's Secret Revelation," which led to an invitation in 1899 to speak to a gathering of Theosophists on the topic of Nietzsche.

In 1902, Steiner became president of the newly formed German section of the Theosophical Society, which was informed by the principles of Alexandrian Neo-Platonic philosophy and Christian mysticism. Steiner eventually translated theosophical ideals into what he called anthroposophy, a scientific approach to esotericism upon which he founded the Anthroposophic Society in 1912. In 1923, Steiner reinstated the society as a response to the social and spiritual challenges posed by World War I and what he perceived as a need for a spiritually oriented scientific approach, including a spiritual science of agriculture (Thomas 2005, 1596).

Steiner's spiritual science of agriculture was most clearly articulated in his 1924 lectures, "Spiritual Foundations for the Renewal of Agriculture" – also referred to as *The Agriculture Lectures* – that were given over a ten-day period in Koberwitz, Silesia, then Eastern Europe, as part of an educational course for farmers who had begun to observe a degradation of land health due to chemical fertilizers. Already familiar with the basic ideas of Steiner's spiritual philosophy of Anthroposophy, the farmers were interested in learning techniques for replenishing the vitality and strength of their livestock and crops. The courses were not meant to teach specific farming practices but to supplement them with a spiritual framework for understanding and connecting with the forces that permeated the Earth and its beings and oriented the cosmos.

Central to Steiner's thought was the idea that the more obvious outer technical world corresponded with a nonobvious inner spiritual world that could be discovered through a method of scientific investigation that heightened ones perception of the forces of nature (Thomas 2005, 1596–97). To teach how this could be achieved, Steiner used detailed drawings in his lectures. In one such drawing he explained the spiritual quality of soil: "We usually think of the soil – which I'm going to indicate here with this line [Drawing 2] – as being something purely mineral, with organic matter coming into it only incidentally to the extent that humus develops or manure is applied. That the soil might contain not only this sort of life, but also an inherent plant-like vitality, and even something of the nature of soul-qualities, this is not even conceived of, much less accepted as fact." (Steiner 1924, 1993, 28) Other drawings depicted the "cosmic constellation" of individual plants, the "cosmic force" of the sun in a plant's leaves, the "ego-potential" of animal manure, and the "etheric principle" of all living beings.

Through meditation, Steiner believed, farmers could become "ever more receptive to the revelations of nitrogen," a central element in biodynamic farming methods (29). The type of meditation conducted in the West, in Europe, he wrote, was different than that conducted in the East. Only "indirectly dependent on the breathing process; we live in the rhythm of concentration and mediation" (55). Still, Steiner's method of meditation did have a bodily component, although he considered it to be "very delicate and subtle" (55). "While meditating, we retain somewhat more carbon dioxide than we do in a state of normal waking consciousness…We don't thrust the full force of the carbon dioxide out there, into the environment that is filled with nitrogen. We hold some back" (55). During the process, Steiner observed, "Everything becomes known, including everything that lives in nitrogen" (55). Once this occurred, the farmer suddenly came to "know all kinds of things…know all about the mysteries at work on the land and around the farm" (29–30).

Steiner saw his spiritual science as providing an urgently needed counterpoint to the materialist agriculture of his day. The latter he equated with an attempt to understand the totality of the human body by studying a little finger. A spiritual approach to agriculture, on the other hand, would seek to understand the interrelationships of the cosmos. So too it would seek connections with the elemental spirits and souls of the plant and animal kingdoms. This way, Steiner believed, a farm could become a thriving, self-sustaining entity.

Bailey's Holy Earth

Writing some 20 years after Steiner and in the U.S. context, Liberty Hyde Bailey wrote similarly to Steiner about a spirituality of nature that developed through people's direct contact with Earth, rather than through religious dogma or belief. "The good spiritual reaction to nature is not a form of dogmatism or impressionism," he wrote in *This Holy Earth*, rather, "[i]t results normally from objective experience, when the person is ready for it and has good digestion" (Bailey 1943, 2008, 53). Like Steiner, Bailey grew-up in the countryside, where he spent a significant amount of time outdoors. Born in South Haven, Michigan in 1848 to Liberty Hyde Bailey, Sr. and Sarah Harrison, the Bailey's were pioneers, living off the land and settling a farm on 80 acres at the mouth of the Black River where the soil was excellent for growing fruit.

The Bailey farm eventually became renowned for its apples, with young Bailey playing an integral role in the orchard's work as he in his youth became well known and sought after by neighbors for his grafting skills. Based on this experience, Bailey coined the term *cultivar*, a well-known term in horticultural and agricultural studies. Bailey went onto study botany at the Michigan Agricultural College (now Michigan State University), and, through the recommendation of his professor William James Beal, became the herbarium assistant to renowned Harvard botanist Asa Gray. From there, Bailey founded and became dean of the Agricultural College at Cornell University where he was influential in creating the cooperative extension system, 4-H, the nature-study movement, and the study of horticulture and rural sociology. In 1908, he became chair of The National Commission on Country Life under President Theodore Roosevelt, a commission charged with the task of revitalizing America's agricultural heritage. Bailey was a prolific writer and published 63 books and edited 100 others, over 100 scientific papers, and 1,300 articles on a variety of subjects, including philosophy and the arts.

Part of the breadth of his work includes a series of five books known as the "Background Books" or the "Philosophy of the Holy Earth series." The best known of the series' titles is its first volume, *The Holy Earth* (1915). In it, Bailey draws on what might be considered more conventional readings of the bible than Steiner. The first section of *The Holy Earth* quotes the opening text of the Hebrew bible: "In the beginning God created the heaven and the earth." Bailey interprets the scripture in the following terms: "This is a statement of tremendous reach, introducing the cosmos; for it sets forth in the fewest words the elemental fact that the formation of the created earth lies above and before man, and that therefore it is not man's but God's. Man finds himself upon it, with many other creatures, all parts in some system which, since it is beyond man and superior to him, is divine" (4).

For Bailey, the Earth was a holy system "because the Earth, and everything that was initially in it, was the product of divine creation" (Taggart , Preface to Bailey 1943, 2008, viii). Different from Steiner's pantheistic view that the divine was in some sense embedded and active in the material universe, Bailey held a deist view of the relationship between God and nature – whereby God created the Earth and then "let it go" so to speak – which allowed an adherence to Darwinian evolution in a way that Steiner's theology did not. Nonetheless, Bailey like Steiner saw the need for a farmer to be a spiritual person in order to rightly see the land and how to cooperate with it. "A man cannot be a good farmer unless he is a religious man," Bailey wrote (Bailey 1943, 2008, 24). "Into this secular and more or less technical education we are now to introduce the element of moral obligation, that the man may understand his peculiar contribution and responsibility to society; but his result cannot be attained until the farmer and every one of us recognize the holiness of the earth" (25–26).

Carver's Earth as God's workshop

Popularly referred to as "the peanut man," George Washington Carver is best known for his scientific genius inventing hundreds of uses for the peanut, from soap to ink to candy. Such a characterization, however, is misleading, as scholars have shown, for it overshadows Carver's broader impact on the development of nature-oriented agricultural techniques. As Carver archivist, John S. Ferrell notes, "In his efforts to develop products from renewable raw materials, his attitude toward waste, and his advocacy of natural farming methods, he presaged current efforts to build an eco-logically sound future" (Ferrell 2007, 11).

Carver was born a slave, likely in the year 1864 or 1865, in Diamond Grove, Missouri, where his mother Mary was owned by Moses and Susan Carver, Ohio-born settlers who were among the first to homestead the area in the 1830s.[7] A par-ticularly tumultuous time in the Civil War, southwestern Missouri faced intense Union and Confederate fighting and frequent attacks in the area by marauders. In a raid of the Carver household not long after George was born, attackers kidnapped George and his mother and took them to Arkansas where they were sold to other masters. Moses Carver attempted to locate both Mary and George, but was only able to recover George, who he bought back for $300. George was raised by the Carvers, as was his older brother, Jim, who worked with Moses in the fields while George worked with "Aunt Susan" doing household work and in the garden. Through this work Carver developed a special fondness and skill for caring for plants. He secretly built a garden with wildflowers transplanted from the woods that surrounded the farm, as flower gardening was viewed at the time as a waste of time and energy. "Day after day," Carver wrote in one reflection "I spent in the woods alone in order to collect my floral beautis [sic]" (Kremer 2011, 7). He became known in the com-munity as the "plant doctor" with neighbors coming to him for advice with ailing plants. Carver cared so deeply for plants, that he called them his "pets," recounting in one instance: "many are the tears I have shed because I would break the roots or flower of some of my pets while removing them from the ground" (8).

After attending a secondary school for blacks in the county seat of Neosho, approximately eight miles from the Carver farm, George was accepted at Highland College in Highland, Kansas, though when he arrived on campus was told that they did not allow black students. He then went to study piano and art at Simpson College in Indianola, Iowa, where one of his teachers recognized his aptitude for painting plants and flowers, and advised him to go study botany at Iowa State Agricultural College in Ames. He entered in 1891 as the first black student, and after graduation stayed on to do a master's degree where his research at the Iowa Experimental Station on plant mycology and pathology thrust him into the national spotlight as a world-class botanist. In 1896, Carver was invited by Booker T. Washington, president of the Tuskegee Institute, to head the university's agriculture department, where Carver stayed for 47 years, developing innovative agricultural education approaches such as the "Jessup Wagon" which traveled from farmstead to farmstead to teach farmers new techniques.

As Carver's notoriety grew, he increasingly traveled to promote the work of the Tuskegee Institute, U.S. peanut production, and racial accord. In one such public event in 1923, a year before Steiner delivered his *Agriculture Lectures*, Carver spoke explicitly about his outlook on the relationship between his personal spiritual experience and his method of doing science. Given to a large audience attending the Women's Board of Domestic Missions at Marble Collegiate Church in downtown Manhattan, Carver told attendees: "I never have to grope for methods: the method is revealed at the moment I am inspired to create something new" (Kremer 2011, 116). Two days later, the *New York Times* ran an editorial entitled "Men of Science Never Talk that Way," calling into question Carver's scientific approach, his race, and the Tuskegee Institute where he was on the faculty. Carver in turn responded in a letter to the Times expressing his regret "that such a gross misunderstanding should arise to what was meant by 'Divine inspiration.' Inspiration is never at variance with information; in fact, the more information one has, the greater will be the inspiration" (Kremer 1991, 129). Carver went on to list his credentials as a graduate of two degrees in scientific agriculture from Iowa State College of Agriculture and Mechanical Arts, as well as the renowned scholars in chemistry and botany who had influenced him. He closed the letter with a scriptural text: "John 8–32, 'And ye shall know the truth and the truth shall make you free.'" "Science is simply the truth about anything" (130).

Carver, like Steiner and Bailey, viewed science and religion as compatible, writing often about his spiritual relationship with the natural world which he saw as infused with divine power. He wrote that he loved "to think of Nature as unlimitless broadcasting stations, through which God speaks to us every day, every hour, and every moment of our lives, if we will only tune in and do so" (143). Carver was a strong advocate of the nature-study movement that Bailey helped to initiate, and worked to develop curriculum for children about how to incorporate nature study with the development of school-based vegetable gardens. He believed that deeper knowledge about the intricacies and workings of the natural world would lead to better farming practices. "The highest attainments in agriculture can be reached only when we clearly understand the mutual relationship between the animal, mineral, and vegetable kingdoms, and how utterly impossible it is for one to exist in a highly organized state without the other" (143). Conversely, where ecological relationships were ignored in agriculture, the land suffered. "Conservation is one of our big problems in this section," Carver was quoted by an Atlanta newspaper in 1940 (Ferrell 2007, 23). "It is a travesty to burn our woods and thereby burn up the fertilizer nature has provided for us. We must enrich our soil every year instead of merely depleting it. It is fundamental that nature will drive away those who commit sins against it" (23).

Carver's mystical relationship with the natural world appeared to grow with age. Like Steiner, Carver often referenced the importance of childhood experiences of nature, including his own, and how it impacted a lifelong affinity for nature. In a 1930 letter he wrote:

> We get closer to God as we get more intimately and understandingly with the things he has created. I know of nothing more inspiring than that of making discoveries for ones self...the singing birds, the buzzing bees, the opening flower, and the budding trees, along with other forms of animate and inanimate matter, all have their marvelous creation story to tell each searcher of truth...We doubt if there is a normal boy or girl in all christendom endowed with the five senses who have not watched with increased interest and profit, the various forms, movements and the gorgeous paintings of the butterfly, many do not know, but will study with increased enthusiasm the striking analogy its life bears to the human soul.
>
> *(Kremer 1991, 142)*

He concluded that as people came "closer and closer in touch with nature" were they "able to see the Divine." That way, they became "fitted to interpret correctly the various languages spoken by all forms of nature" (143).

Carver's approach blends Steiner's pantheism and Bailey's deism into a form of nature spirituality where the divine is understood transcendentally and immanently in relation to the Earth. In her essay, "York, Harriet, and George: Writing African American Ecological Ancestors," Kimberly Ruffin interprets Carver's spirituality as a religious syncretism between Christianity and traditional African religion. She quotes Toni Morrison on the topic: "I [Morrison] could blend the acceptance of the supernatural and a profound rootedness in the real world at the same time with neither taking precedence over the other. It is indicative of the cosmology, the way in which Black people looked at the world. We are very practical people, very down-to-earth, even shrewd people. But within that practicality we also accepted what I suppose could be call superstition and magic, which is another way of knowing things" (as cited in Ruffin 2007, 47).

Taken together Steiner's, Bailey's, and Carvers' spiritual conceptions of agriculture suggest a view of Earth's sacred, or in Bailey's terms holy worth, by virtue of its relation to a divine being or force in the universe. Moreover, in their conceptions the conservation of Earth's sacred systems and processes "trump" human use in the sense that the mutual relationships among beings ought to be considered the more significant unit of concern, ecologically, morally, and spiritually. Despite such a holistic view, Steiner, Bailey, and Carver see sacred value in and the need for attentive concern toward the tiniest units in nature, including, in Steiner's case, the nitrogen in soil. The ethical upshot of these views is that people, especially farmers, need to learn to live in "sincere relations" (Bailey) with the company of others. To do this, agriculturalists must develop a spiritual practice in relation to the natural world – in Steiner's terms, meditation; in Bailey's and Carver's conceptions, routine, direct contact with the land.

Intimations of soil as sacred religion

Spotlighting Steiner's, Bailey's, and Carver's views helps illuminate some of the sensibilities embedded in what I perceive as an emergent form of agroecological spirituality in the United States. Such spirituality has overlaps with what religion scholar, Bron Taylor (2009) has termed "dark green religion," the belief that Earth is in some sense sacred and therefore worthy of reverent care. Different from Taylor's conception, soil as sacred spirituality is shaped explicitly by the agricultural context and experience. Soil as sacred spirituality can take on supernaturalistic or naturalistic forms, even within the context of the Abrahamic traditions and communities emphasized in this book.

So, for example, as we will see in subsequent chapters, an African–American congregationally supported agriculture project in Chicago, Illinois, Mother Carr's Organic Farm, interprets its organic agricultural methods as mimicking natural process and systems as "God intended," providing a kind of faithful practice for congregants to serve God and the community. Coastal Roots Farm, a Jewish farm in Encinitis, California, combines ancient Jewish rituals and biodynamic farming methods as a way to foster and narrate spiritual and agricultural practices that connect people to Earth's seasonal cycles. Abundant Table in Thousand Oaks, California holds weekly Farm Church gatherings that emphasize the importance of spiritual contemplation in developing a moral relationship with the land and the production and eating of food.

Even as these examples, along with Steiner's, Bailey's, and Carver's conceptions, *do* tend to involve supernatural beliefs in a divine creator, the ethical and ecological imperative to conserve the land community appears to be the more significant principle. What will be important to examine moving forward is how spiritual and moral interpretations of food and agriculture are contemporarily being adapted by individuals and groups to make sense of and to live sustainably within shifting ecological circumstances. Furthermore, what we will want to learn is the extent to which these religious interpretations are being considered in broader public conversations about moral significance of current agricultural and food practices. While empirical investigation of this latter phenomenon is beyond this book's scope, the question looms in the background, for as I have already stated, one of the book's contentions is that the neglect of religious and spiritual perspectives and narratives in scholarly and societal discussions of agricultural and food ethics has been detrimental to developing a more fully representative dialogue around some of today's most pressing environmental problems. Thus, in this next chapter we move onto consider the plurality of contemporary religious views that have been put forward regarding one of agriculture's most highly debated issues – that of genetically modified organisms.

Notes

1 Vandana Shiva observes in the documentary, *Dirt! The Movie* (2009) that traditionally everything in India was made from soil, from pottery to houses and buildings to the mixture used to clean floors made of dirt.
2 For the information on current levels of soil degradation I am indebted to the following studies referenced on the website, "Food, Energy, & Water: Environmental Issues from a Global Perspective" (FEW), www.fewresources.org/soil-science-and-society-were-running-out-of-dirt.html (accessed October, 2016); David Pimentel, "Soil Erosion: A Food and Environmental Threat," *Journal of the Environment, Development and Sustainability* (2006); Philippe Rekacewicz, "Global Soil Degradation," International assessment of agricultural science and technology for development (2008); David Pimentel and Mario Giampietro, *Food, Land, Population and the U.S. Economy* (1994).
3 See FEW website, www.fewresources.org/soil-science-and-society-were-running-out-of-dirt.html (accessed October, 2016).
4 David Pimentel, "Population Growth and the Environment: Planetary Stewardship," Dec. 1998. Cited on FEW website, www.fewresources.org/soil-science-and-society-were-running-out-of-dirt.html (accessed October, 2016).
5 See, for example, explications of Carver's work in *Land and Power: Sustainable Agriculture and African Americans* (2007).
6 Steiner is also known in the religion and ecology literature for his spiritualization of Ernst Haekel's Darwinian-based pantheistic philosophy. See Taylor (2009, 156).
7 I am indebted to Gary R. Kremer's biography (2011) of George Washington Carver for the history of Carver's early life that follows.

References

Bailey, L.H. (1943, 2008) *The Holy Earth*, with Preface by R.E.Taggart, Michigan State University Press, East Lansing, MI.
Berry, W. (1977) *The Unsettling of America: Culture and Agriculture*, Sierra Club Books, San Francisco, CA.
Common Ground Media, Inc.; a film by B. Benenson and G. Rosow; produced by B. Benenson, G. Rosow, E. Dailly; directed by B. Benenson and G. Rosow; co-director, E. Dailly. (2009). Dirt!: the movie. [U.S.]: presented by Common Ground Media.
Emerson, R.W. (1844) "Nature," in *Emerson's Essays* (1926, 1961), with an introduction by I.Edman,Thomas Crowell, NewYork, NY, 380–401.
Ferrell, J.S. (2007) "George Washington Carver: A blazer of trails to a sustainable future" in Jordan, J.L., Pennick, E., Hill, W.A., and Zabawa, R. (eds.), *Land and Power: Sustainable Agriculture and African Americans*, Sustainable Agriculture Publications, Waldorf, MD, 11–32.
Hillel, D.J. (1991) *Out of the Earth: Civilization and the Life of the Soil*, The Free Press, New York, NY.
Jordan, J.L., Pennick, E., Hill,W.A., and Zabawa, R. (eds.) (2007) *Land and Power: Sustainable Agriculture and African Americans*, Sustainable Agriculture Publications, Waldorf, MD.
Kellogg, C.E. (1941) *The Soils that Support Us: An Introduction to the Study of Soils and Their Use by Men*, The Macmillan Company, NewYork, NY.

Kirschenmann, F. (2004) "A Brief History of Sustainable Agriculture," *Science and Environmental Health Network*. Available at www.sehn.org/Volume_9-2.html (accessed March 2, 2016).

Kremer, G.R. (ed.) (1991) *George Washington Carver: In His Own Words*, University of Missouri Press, Columbia, MO.

Kremer, G.R. (2011) *George Washington Carver: A Biography*, Greenwood, Santa Barbara, CA.

Leopold, A. (1949, 1987) *A Sand County Almanac: And Sketches Here and There*, Oxford University Press, New York, NY.

Lindbo, D., Kozlowski, D., and Robinson, C. (eds.) (2012) *Know Soil Know Life*, Soil Science Society of America, Madison, WI.

Logan, W.B. (1995) *Dirt: The Ecstatic Skin of the Earth*, Riverhead Books, New York, NY.

Lowdermilk, W.C. (1940) "The Eleventh Commandment," *American Forests* 46:1940, 12–15.

Özdemir, I. (2003) "Toward an Understanding of Environmental Ethics from a Qur'anic Perspective," in R.C. Foltz, F.M. Denny, and A. Baharuddin (eds.), *Islam and Ecology: A Bestowed Trust*, Harvard University Press, Cambridge, MA, 3–38.

Ruffin, K. (2007) "York, Harriet, and George: Writing African American Ecological Ancestors," in Jordan, J.L., Pennick, E., Hill, W.A., and Zabawa, R. (eds.), *Land and Power: Sustainable Agriculture and African Americans*, Sustainable Agriculture Publications, Waldorf, MD, 33–56.

Steiner, R. (1924, 1993) *Spiritual Foundations for the Renewal of Agriculture*. Creeger, Catherine E. and Gardner, Malcom (trans). Gardner, Malcom (ed.), Bio-Dynamic Farming and Gardening Association, Inc., Kimberton, PA, 310.

Taggart, R.E. (2008) Preface to L.H. Bailey (1943, 2008) *The Holy Earth*, Michigan State University Press, East Lansing, MI, vii–ix.

Taylor, B.R. (2009) *Dark Green Religion: Nature Spirituality and the Planetary Future*, University of California Press, Berkeley, CA.

Thomas, N.C. (2005) "Steiner, Rudolf – and anthroposophy," in B.R. Taylor (ed.), *Encyclopedia of Religion and Nature*, Continuum, New York, NY, 1596–97.

Thompson, P.B. (1995) *Spirit of the Soil: Agriculture and Environmental Ethics*, Routledge, New York, NY.

Wirzba, N. (2011) *Food and Faith: A Theology of Eating*, Cambridge University Press, New York, NY.

3

PLANTS

The power and miracle of seeds

Perhaps no other issue in agricultural and food ethics has received greater attention than that of genetically modified organisms (GMOs). Debates range from those who argue that the manipulation of genes in plants and animals represents a form of "playing God" to those who worry that GM foods pose uncertain consequences for human health and ecosystem integrity and biodiversity. Other concerns revolve around issues of human population growth and food security, climate change, global markets and patents, labeling, the role of agribusiness, and impacts on farmers and the poor. Philosophers, citizen groups, and presidential commissions have issued multiple, diverse, and extensive ethical analyses and recommendations related to the issues. But how have religious thinkers and communities contributed to the conversation?

This chapter evaluates a variety of religious responses to GMOs, including those that argue for and against genetic food production. In particular, it focuses on the genetic modification of seeds and plants since these are the entities that have elicited the greatest response in Jewish, Christian, and Muslim thought and activism. My main purpose is not to argue for one side or the other, as the issues are much too context specific and multidimensional for that. Rather, what I hope to show is just how varied and diverse are religious viewpoints on the ethical permissibility of GM foods. I take this approach not as an avoidance strategy, but rather as a way to "thicken" the discussion within the study of food ethics and within broader public debate on the topic. In the end, I highlight some of the ways in which religious farms are working to recover spiritual meanings and narratives about seeds' sacred qualities.

Strands of the debate over GMOs

The manipulation of species for human consumptive purposes has been occurring for thousands of years. Still, much of the manipulation that occurs today differs dramatically in terms of the specificity with which genetic material can be moved and synthesized to create altered or even entirely new organisms. GMOs involve the transferring of genetic material, or DNA (deoxyribonucleic acid), from one organism, bacterium, plant, or animal to another species. It may also involve the blocking or removal of a particular gene. Among the first genetically modified fruits introduced to the U.S. market, Calgene's Flavr Savr tomato, for example, added the antisense gene, APH(3')II (aminoglycoside 3'-phosphotransferase II), in order to slow the tomatoes ripening process and resist rotting.

Since the mid-1990s, the volume of GM crops grown worldwide has increased exponentially. From 1996 to 2003 alone, global land use for GM crops increased from 4 to 167 million acres. Ninety nine percent of these GM crops contain a pest or herbicide resistant quality, allowing farmers to use pesticides and herbicides more discriminately and efficiently. Ninety nine percent of the world's GM crops are planted in the United States, Brazil, Argentina, Canada, China, and South Africa, with two-thirds of them planted in the United States. Despite the fact that GM crops are often touted as the magic bullet for solving hunger in the global South, they represent only about two percent of plantings on arable land in these countries (Singer and Mason 2006, 208).

Several sets of concerns have predominated the ethical debate over GM foods. These include worries about the status of nonhuman organisms, consequences for human and ecosystem health and biodiversity, the role of markets and patents, labeling and consumer choice, and impacts on farmers and farming communities.[1] Prior to examining responses to these issues as they have developed within the Abrahamic traditions, let us consider some of the most pressing arguments that have been put forward in the wider public debate.

Human and ecological health

In *The Ethics of What We Eat: Why Our Food Choices Matter* (2006), philosopher Peter Singer and environmental writer Jim Mason trace the moral problem of GM plants through the lens of a vegan family, the Farbs. The Farbs are committed to avoiding GM foods as much as possible, given what they perceive as the risks to long-term human and ecological health. Since the United States does not require the labeling of GM foods, the Farbs focus on purchasing organic and non-corn- and soy-based foods. One of the most widely grown GM crops is Bt. Corn, a variety of corn that is inserted with a bacterium (*Bacillus thuringiensis*) that generates a protein in every cell of the corn plant that is toxic to moths, making it so that farmers do not have to spray for the common pest, the corn-borer. Opponents of Bt. Corn view its built-in pesticide as posing potentially harmful long-term consequences to humans, as well as other creatures and ecosystems. Joann Farb's view is typical of such a stance. GM foods such as Bt. Corn, she states, introduce "novel, potentially toxic, proteins" that the human species "has had no biological experience with" (Singer and Mason 2006, 208–9).

Proponents of GM crops counter that the varieties currently being grown and the foods derived from them are safe for human consumption. Most scientists agree with this position notes a report issued by the United Nations' Food and Agriculture Organization (FAO): "the transgenic crops currently being grown and the foods derived from them are safe to eat" (as cited in Singer and Mason 2006, 210). This is despite the fact, the FAO report also notes, that "little is known about their long-term effects" (210). Additionally, proponents of GM foods such as the International Council for Science often emphasize the fact that just because GM foods have thus far been found safe for human consumption it "does not guarantee that no risks will be encountered as more foods are developed with novel characteristics" (210). Princeton molecular biologist Lee Silver therefore concludes: "Each GM modification has to be considered on a case-by-case regulatory basis. I would want to see the theory and empirical data on any other GM crop before making any claims about safety" (210).

The Farbs, as with those living in the United States more generally, emphasize the potential human health risks of GM foods. European scientists and citizens, however, have more readily emphasized the issues of the intrinsic value of organisms and risks to biodiversity and natural systems. Echoing earlier debates about the ethics of human genetic manipulation, European debates have questioned whether GMOs represent a form of "playing God," overstepping human boundaries in relation to the nonhuman created order. At stake in these arguments are understandings about what constitutes the "natural" and the "cultural" and how these spheres should interface in the context of agriculture. Furthermore, they underscore the role of human responsibilities with regard to the application of agbiotechnology, and raise questions about the values, virtues, and norms that should guide individuals and societies in developing GM related endeavors.

Feeding a growing global population on a warming planet

Whether the potential human and ecological risks of GM crops are outweighed by the need to feed a growing global human population, particularly the hungry poor, is another ethical issue that Singer and Mason raise. "What about the developing world," they ask, "where a billion people cannot be sure they and their families will have enough to eat? Would it not be justified to take a greater risk for their sake?" (214). GM crops have the potential to reduce the need for water in drought-ravaged countries as well as the need for expensive pesticides that poor farmers often cannot afford. This makes some argue that in certain contexts, particularly in Africa, the genetic modification of plants is necessary in order to sustain agricultural production.

Still others take the position that GM crops are neither necessary nor desirable to feed the world's growing population. Czech–Canadian scientist and policy analyst Vaclav Smil, for instance, insists that the world's projected population of nine billion people, a number believed to level off by 2050, can be fed without resorting to the use of GM technologies. There are numerous well-tested ways of improving agricultural practices that do not assume the potential long-term health and ecological risks associated with GM foods, according to Smil. It is the corporate driven

agbiotechnology system that is to blame for the problems that plagu
and farmers, go arguments such as these. Central here are critique
globalization and the free-market policies of the international finan
(IFIs), namely, the World Trade Organization (WTO) and Internati
Fund (IMF). It is worth elaborating for how some religious group
heavily on this issue in particular.[2]

Intellectual property rights and seed patenting

Established in the early 1990s, based on the Uruguay Round of the General
Agreement on Tariffs and Trade (GATT), some environmental activists, including
in the food and faith movement, have argued that the policies of the IFIs are an
extension of the destructive ecological agricultural policies developed during the
Green Revolution beginning in the 1940s. The Green Revolution was a massive
effort undertaken by a group of scientists and political and business leaders to transfer the technologies, tools, and techniques of Western agriculture to the developing
world so to increase crop yields and end world hunger. Critics argue that the results
of Green Revolution policies have not only failed to increase the scale of yields
promised, they have forced farmers in the global South to adopt technologies that
they could not afford, which has ultimately undercut local and regional capacities
to cultivate food.

WTO rules force countries in the global South to adopt policies such as intellectual property rights (IPRs) and seed patent laws that benefit multinational corporations (MNCs) rather than citizens and farmers. The "Trade Related Intellectual
Property Rights Agreement of the World Trade Organization (WTO), allow corporations to usurp the knowledge of the seed and monopolize it by claiming it as
their private property," writes Shiva. "Over time, this results in corporate monopolies over the seed itself" (Shiva 2000, 8–9). In India, Shiva notes, farmers over
centuries have developed 200,000 varieties of rice, including Basmati, brown, and
black rice and saline-resistant rice that is able to grow in coastal waters, with some
varieties that are grown in floodwaters that can reach 18 feet high. Yet corporations
like RiceTec of the United States are claiming patents on Basmati rice that has been
evolved by peasant Indian farmers. Soybean and mustard crops that originated in
East Asia are now "owned" (patented) by Monsanto and Calgene respectively. Seeds
and plants that have been evolved over centuries of innovations by resident farmers
are being "hijacked," as Shiva puts it, by a handful of global agribusinesses through
intellectual property rights regimes, a phenomena Shiva refers to as "seed piracy."

The market consolidation of seed has increased significantly in the past decade.
When Shiva wrote Stolen Harvest in 2000, she noted that ten corporations controlled 32 percent of the commercial seed market (which was then valued at 23 billion dollars) and 100 percent of the market for transgenic or GM seeds. These same
corporations controlled the global agrochemical and pesticide market. Today, just
five major seed companies control the global commercial seed market: Monsanto,
Syngenta, Bayer, Dow, and DuPont. Combined, these five corporations acquired

more than 200 other companies between 1996 and 2008, as shown in a study by agronomist Phillip Howard (2009). It is not just the vertical concentration of seed consolidation that is of concern to thinkers such as Shiva, it is also the horizontal, additional integrated international institutional and corporate related policies that are at stake. Consider how Technology Use Agreements (TUAs) are used by global seed corporations. TUAs are a type of license that is needed in order to use a patented product. In agriculture, a TUA is "a contract specifying that farmers do not own the seed, that they just grow it under a contract and have to deliver all the grain in accordance with [the seed company's] wishes" (as cited in Wilson 2002, 156). Monsanto's TUA for farmers states the following. Farmers are 1) required to plant the commercial crop for only one season; 2) to not supply any of the protected seed to anyone else for planting; 3) to not use the seed or provide it to anyone for crop-breeding or research; 4) to spray only with 'Roundup' (also manufactured by Monsanto) if using a glyphosate-based herbicide" (Wilson 2002, 156).

Such form of corporate control over how a farmer uses and distributes seed is a type of war against farmers and the land, argues Shiva. In the Indian context, she writes, the seeds of the Green Revolution for which Norman Borlaug received the Nobel Peace Prize became in just two decades the seeds of war in the Indian Punjab. Shiva explains:

> 1984 was a dramatic and tragic year for India. It was the year the violence in Punjab, which claimed thirty thousand lives, reached its climax, with the army entering the Golden Temple in June to wipe out the extremists, and with Prime Minister Indira Gandhi being assassinated in retaliation. It was also the year of the Bhopal tragedy in which three thousand were killed by a leak from a Union Carbide pesticide plant. Thousands were crippled for life. And in the summer of 1984, Karnataka experienced drought, in spite of normal rainfall. The drought was created by the Green Revolution's 'miracle' seeds that reduced biomass, creating a fodder famine and depleting organic matter in the soil. Soils, starved of organic matter that the tall indigenous sorghum varieties provided, could no longer store the rainfall as soil moisture, and drought and desertification resulted from a short-term, narrow-minded search for high yields of grain.
>
> *(Shiva 2003, 121–22)*

Shiva writes that it was during that drought that she began to understand the deep connection between the cultivation of native seeds and ecological health and security. From there she discovered the writings of Wendell Berry, where she came to see that, "The unsettling of India was repeating the pattern of the unsettling of America" (122). In 1987, Shiva founded the seed saving and organic producers network and organization, Navdanya, which means "nine seeds" and "new gift." Since then, Navdanya has facilitated the development of 122 community seed banks across India, trained over five million farmers in seed sovereignty, food sovereignty and sustainable agriculture, and helped create India's largest direct marketing, fair trade organic network. "In today's context of biological and ecological destruction," states Navdanya's literature, "seed savers are the true givers of seed. This gift or 'dana' of Navadhanyas (nine seeds) is the ultimate gift – it is a gift of life, of heritage and continuity. Conserving seed is conserving biodiversity, conserving knowledge of the seed and its utilization, conserving culture, conserving sustainability."[3] Navdanya's work echoes the themes of seeds' spiritual meanings highlighted at this chapter's end. For now, however, we continue our examination of the ethics of GM foods by looking at some of the main arguments issued by thinkers and activists in Jewish, Christian, and Muslim traditions.

Religious perspectives on GMOs

Even as religious treatments of GMOs have tended to follow the types of ethical arguments just noted, what distinguishes them are the types of sources and narratives they draw on to make them. Moreover, even as Jewish, Christian, and Islamic traditions share certain beliefs about God, nature, and human beings there is nevertheless no consensus among or within these traditions on the ethical permissibility of GM foods.[4] Thus, in this section we look at a variety of religious positions that have been put forward in relation to the problem of GMOs, including those articulated by religious leaders and activist groups in addition to academic theologians and religion scholars. My intent is not to give a comprehensive review, rather to underscore the plurality of types of responses that have emerged in the past decade and a half especially.

We begin with viewpoints that condone, or at least do not outright disallow the possibility of the development of GM foods. Central to this line of thinking is the theological belief that humans, as made in the image of God, are created as God's partners in working toward a more peaceable and just world. Insofar as GM foods are perceived as helping to do that, they are understood to be theologically and ethically acceptable. An example of this view can be seen in a piece by Rabbi Akiva Wolff written for the Jerusalem Center for Public Affairs. Appealing to Jewish law (*halakhah*), Wolff suggests that genetic engineering is morally acceptable as long as human life is improved and the global food supply is increased. On the biblical prohibition of *kilayim*, or mixing of different species of animals and plants, Wolff argues that God does not prohibit the genetic modification of food crops. He concludes, "man may manipulate the creation, but only within certain limitations – these being defined by the natural and religious laws given by the Creator. The defining ethical criteria is that all of the legally permitted actions must bring the world closer to perfection and not further away" (Wolff 2001).

Islam scholar, Fatima Agha al-Hayani similarly argues that agbiotechnological applications in developing GM foods are permissible in Islam insofar as religious ethical principles are upheld. She writes: "there exists no conflict between science and Islam. However, this acquired knowledge is a responsibility and a trust, given and accepted by the human, to be applied to the betterment of humankind: to do good deeds and to prevent evil. It must be accompanied by compassion, kindness,

[margin handwritten note: ? magnets on how much wealth]

and generosity" (al-Hayani 2007, 159). al-Hayani further suggests that Muslims have a duty and responsibility to pursue scientific research related to genetic engineering, especially if it can help alleviate global hunger and aid the poor, an issue, she writes, that is of upmost importance in Islam. The main *halal* certification organization in North America, the Islamic Food and Nutrition Council of America (IFANCA), has taken the stance of what Islamic studies scholar, Ebrahim Moosa calls "manageable risk," stating that there is no reason that GMO foods cannot be *halal* or permissible, as long as the GMO does not come from *haram* or forbidden sources. As within Judaism, nevertheless, there is debate over whether a gene taken from say pig genetic materials and inserted into a new organism would render it forbidden given the prohibition on eating pork within Jewish and Muslim dietary codes. On this Moosa writes: "Obviously opinions would be divided on these questions depending on a range of factors. Among these factors would be the way adherents understand the moral commandments of their faith, their meritorious view of science or otherwise, and the way in which certain realities get communicated to them" (Moosa 2009, 144).

Official statements of the Roman Catholic Church have tended to support GM technologies when it comes to food production, even as Pope Francis' 2015 encyclical, *Laudato si' ('Praise Be to You'): On Care for our Common Home* is more cautious. Catholic theological views that have favored genetic modification have emphasized the divine role of science in bringing about God's will in the world. Cardinal Renato Martino, leader of the Pontifical Council for Justice and Peace based at the Vatican stated in 2003 that the Catholic Church supported GM foods as a response to global hunger because "scientific progress was part of the divine plan" (as cited in Owen 2003). The influential Catholic organization, the Pontifical Academy of Sciences, has come out in favor of agricultural biotechnology as a way to help feed the poor and improve agriculture in the global South. Proceedings from 2001 and 2009 conferences state respectively that agbiotechnology can help "to develop plants that can produce larger yields of healthier food under sustainable conditions with an acceptable level of risk" and "offer food safety and security, better health and environmental sustainability," particularly for the world's poorest people and countries (as cited in Omobowale, Singer, and Daar 2009).

Francis' *On Care for our Common Home* presents a more measured view of the theological permissibility of GM crops, emphasizing the need for ethics to guide agbiotechnological applications especially. It states: "It is difficult to make a general judgment about genetic modification (GM), whether vegetable or animal, medical or agricultural, since these vary greatly among themselves and call for specific considerations. The risks involved are not always due to the techniques used, but rather to their improper or excessive application" (Francis 2015, 39). Where worries about GMOs are expressed in the document they emphasize unknown risks to ecosystems and potential negative impacts on small farmers: "The expansion of these crops has the effect of destroying the complex network of ecosystems, diminishing the diversity of production and affecting regional economies, now and in the future. In various countries, we see an expansion of oligopolies for the production of cereals and other products needed for their cultivation. This dependency would be aggravated were the production of infertile seeds to be considered; the effect would be to force farmers to purchase them from larger producers" (39). Still, Francis is critical of environmentalists who recommend the restriction of GM technologies for ecological reasons, yet fail to do similarly when it comes to human life. The encyclical concludes that what is needed is broad public debate that considers all available information, and includes discussions with the multiplicity of stakeholders impacted by GM related issues, including, farmers, people living near fields, seed producers, consumers, civil authorities, and others.

Jewish ethicist, Laurie Zoloth takes a similarly moderate approach, observing what she calls a "fascinating paradox in Jewish responses to GM food" (Zoloth 2009, 95). On the one hand, writes Zoloth, most Conservative and Orthodox thinkers advocate the widest use of new genetic technologies, even as they uphold a strict reading of Jewish texts, while on the other hand Reform and Reconstructionist thinkers tend to favor a more cautious approach to GM food, even as they generally favor a more liberal and creative reading of texts. Drawing on scientific and Jewish sources, Zoloth in the end sees no intrinsic theological or ethical reasons for disallowing the use of GM technologies in food production. Such technological applications should, nevertheless, be guided by the principle of *kilayim*, which prohibits certain mixtures (e.g., animals that should not be bred, seeds that should not be mixed) and is based on the Jewish belief that creation has a God-given intent and order. Rather than serving as a prohibition of genetic mixing, however, as liberal Jewish thinkers have read it, Zoloth interprets *kilayim* in the context of the biblical texts on mixing (Deuteronomy 22 and Isaiah), which she sees as primarily speaking about farming production in the context of the covenant between God, the land, the Israelites, and the poor. Read this way, stipulations about mixing seeds and animals are meant to insure a divinely designed food system where crops are rotated, planted, and allowed to cease in order for the poor to glean fields' edges. Zoloth uses the example of a scientist working to genetically altar the sub-Saharan African staple food, cassava, so that it is more richly nutritious for inhabitants who suffer high rates of mortality and morbidity due to malnutrition. She concludes that GMO in food production should not be viewed in terms of science fiction hypotheticals, but rather as

> an answer to a world right now, with the poor, right now, waiting their turn in our harvest…GM foods have extraordinary promise…they are like seeds themselves, for the entire thing could fail utterly, defeated unless watched carefully, nurtured through a risky start, and harvested in careful accordance to the laws of justice and responsibility.
>
> *(110)*

Religious views that intrinsically oppose agbiotechnology and GMOs include critiques similar to those already noted by Singer and Mason and Shiva. Emphasizing the principle of social justice, Roman Catholic priest and ecologist Sean McDonagh argues against the view of GM foods issued by the Vatican and Pontifical Academy of the Sciences, stating: "All the experts at Catholic development agencies have taken the position that this is not the way to address food security, and that there's no magic bullet for hunger. What's needed is land reform, financial aid to small-scale farmers, markets where they can get value so they're not caught by the middle man" (Allen 2009). Christian theologian, Norman Wirzba too argues against GM food for ecological reasons. Resonant with the sentiments of Joann Farb noted above, Wirzba worries that GM foods have the potential to "unleash 'genetic pollutants' into our natural habitats and so upset finely tuned balances that keep food chains resilient through time...When we release new genetic material, especially material that would not have developed on its own (a number of our genetic designs cross species barriers), we often have no idea what the adverse affects might be" (Wirzba 2011, 88).

Islam scholar, Mohammad Aslam Parvaiz similarly argues against genetic engineering of nonhuman organisms for ecological reasons. Drawing on the Qur'anic principle of divinely created proportionality and measure in the Earth, Parvaiz writes, "Allah says in the Holy Quar'an that His creations are perfect and flawless. They have been created in harmony and balance with the environment" (Parvaiz 2003, 398). He cites examples of transgenic raised fish escaping into wild ecosystems and polluting native wild fish populations such as happened in Norway and the spread through pollination of herbicide resistant genes in transgenic plants such as canola to weeds such as Brassica and wild mustard which then also become herbicide resistant and much more troublesome.

Jewish arguments against GMOs posed by thinkers such as Rabbi Elihu Gevirtz and the environmental organization TEVA emphasize the idea that humans are partners with God as caretakers of creation, and that GM activities violate that role. Advocating for the labeling of GM foods they state: "What are the values that God would want us to impart? love, justice, truth and beauty. The use of GMOs is a violation of all of those. At the very least, food needs to be labeled, and consumed toward a consciousness of health."[5] Founder of the progressive religious environmental organization, The Shalom Center, Rabbi Arthur Waskow worries that genetic modification is but one problem in a much larger suite of problems posed by the modern industrial food system and environmental crisis. He writes:

> And the world-wide ecological crisis created by the actions of the human race in the last few generations of modernity has begun to raise concerns among Jews as well as other communities, for how to redefine what food is proper and sacred to grown and to eat. Questions about the use of pesticides and of genomic engineering; of the burning of fossil fuels to transport foods across the planet, meanwhile disturbing the whole climatic context in which the foods are grown; the misuse of topsoil and the use of long-term poisonous fertilizers; the effects of massive livestock breeding on the production of a potent global-scorching gas, methane – all these have raised profound new questions.
>
> *(As cited in Zoloth 2009, 93)*

Combining social and ecological critiques, the global ecumenical organization, The World Council of Churches has strongly opposed genetic engineering of plants and animals for food production purposes. "Caring for Life: Genetics, Agriculture and Human Life," a report published in 2005 by its Working Group on Genetic Engineering of the Justice, Peace and Creation concludes that "GE messes with life, messes with truth, messes with our common inheritance (i.e. human culture and biodiversity), messes with justice, messes with human health, messes with the lives of peasant farmers in developing countries and the relationship between human beings and other forms of life." The report further argues that Christians working in the agbiotechnology industry should become whistle-blowers and conscientious objectors to research conducted in the field.

Overall, contemporary responses to the GM debates within the Abrahamic faith traditions are incredibly varied and diverse, and should be taken as such in public dialogue around the issues. Furthermore, much of how the problem of GMOs is understood in religious terms in the Abrahamic faiths hinges ultimately on inter- pretations of the divine in relation to nature and humanity, a note too that should be underscored when theological perspectives on the topic are brought to broader discussions. Despite the plurality of religious arguments on GM foods that have been put forward, curiously missing, nevertheless, in these more analytical theologi- cal arguments is attention to the symbolic narratives about seeds' meanings that can be found among faith groups engaged on the ground with food and farming work. Thus, in this final section we look at some of the ways in which religious farms are spiritually interpreting seeds and the human encounter with them and how such interpretations reflect deeper meanings about God and Earth and its beings.

Narratives of sacred seeds

As with Shiva's Navdanya in the Indian context, seeds hold sacred meaning for many groups working in the food and faith movement in North America. Narratives employed by these groups incorporate hands-on, seed-related experiences with religious teachings and rituals in ways that offer an interesting example of what scholars refer to as "lived religion" or "lived theology."[6] Such interpretations under- score the idea that even in the midst of modern industrial hi-tech culture people continue to find meaning and satisfaction by engaging in simple, land-based prac- tices of the most mundane kind. Below I highlight several types of meanings for seeds as narrated by faith-based farm and food groups.

Seeds as holding and revealing Earth's sacred mysteries

Genesis Farm in Blairstown, New Jersey is one of nine institutions that the Dominican Sisters have developed since their founding in 1881. One of the sisters' key ministries has been seed saving, which founding sister Miriam MacGillis views in both practical and symbolic terms. The sisters work to save heirloom seed stock and promote plant biodiversity, work that they view as also helping to preserve the mystical tradition of Christianity. This is because the sisters see the very substance and activity of a seed as a miracle, a divine mystery that humans ultimately did not create, yet can come to know through hands-on farming work. "The essence of a seed is life," state the sisters. "Through it, generation after generation of wisdom is carried to the present moment for release into the future. The seed is part of an unfolding process. It evolves through the ages in accordance to many forces – some that are known, but many that are ultimately beyond human comprehension" (as cited in Marshall 2013).

Based on their beliefs about seeds' sacred quality, the sisters have fought hard against agbiotechnology corporations such as Monsanto for how it claims ownership over farmers' use of seeds. In March 2011, Genesis Farm joined 60 plaintiffs in filing a lawsuit – Organic Seed Growers and Trade Association [OSGATA] et al. v. Monsanto – that challenged Monsanto's patents on genetically modified seed. By June of 2011, the number of plaintiffs had grown to 83, including 36 organizations, 14 seed companies, and 33 farms and farmers.[7] The organic growers were suing preemptively in order to protect themselves from being accused of patent infringement should their crops ever become accidentally (by, say, wind or animal transfer) contaminated by Monsanto's transgenic seeds. Between 1997 and 2010, Monsanto had already filed 144 lawsuits against U.S. farmers and settled another 700 out of court for this reason. "If a seed represents the deep mysteries of the Universe," the sisters narrate, "then transgenic seed – those that are implanted with genes of another species – represents a violent desecration of that mystery" (as cited in Marshall 2013).

Similar to the philosophy of deep ecology, religious meanings that emphasize the mysteries of the universe that seeds embody privilege what is perceived as "wild" nature, in this case, nature as God originally created it. On this view, the sacred quality of nature is understood as a phenomenon to be discovered, as well as one that can be damaged or degraded, by certain human activities, including, in this case, by interfering in nature's created integrity through genetic manipulation.

Seeds as a metaphor for the spiritual life

In this rendering of seeds' sacred meaning it is the gathering and planting of seeds that marks the cyclical rhythm of the seasons and the symbolic making of seasonal religious rituals. Particularly evident in Jewish food groups that emphasize the ritualization of the food process in tandem with Jewish ceremonies, holidays, and festivals, this theme sees seeds as a metaphor for the spiritual life of faith. Consider a seed saving workshop organized by the Detroit chapter of the progressive Jewish organization, Hazon. Held in the month of Cheshvan in the Hebrew calendar, the workshop emphasized the month's liturgical themes of awaiting growth in the season's coming darkness. In the Torah, the great flood narrated in Genesis (7:10–11) occurred in the season of Cheshvan, which is also the rainy season in Israel. There are no holidays during Cheshvan and accordingly it is interpreted as a time of quiet waiting. Detroit Hazon interpreted seed saving in light of the month of Cheshvan this way: "It's Cheshvan – in our tradition a time for rain, for seeds to be gathered and planted in the growing darkness. You'll place them underground, protected by the dark, the place/time of dreaming, so that the new season can begin again.

In this workshop…we'll gather your real and metaphoric seeds, and come together in community to dream what's next."[8]

Farm manager at the Jewish farm at Leichtag Ranch in Encinitas, California, Daron "Farmer D" Joffe understands seed planting as an exhibition of patient faith and waiting, both of which he interprets in quasi-spiritual terms. In *Citizen Farmers: The Biodynamic Way to Grow Healthy Food, Build Thriving Communities, and Give Back to the Earth* (2014), Joffe has a chapter titled "Sowing=Faith" that represents this view. The chapter opens with a quote by Henry David Thoreau: "The smallest seed of faith is better than the largest fruit of happiness" (Joffe 2014, 89). Joffe continues: "Planting a seed is both an act of independence and a leap of faith. Your crop is always, ultimately, at the mercy of Mother Nature. But there are techniques that will increase your odds of success and maximize your yield. In these pages you will learn the best way to plant seeds and seedlings, utilize space, dig holes, soak seeds, plant by the moon, and irrigate properly and wisely. In the process, you will become a true citizen farmer, as well as more successful with all the seeds you plant in life" (89). Note how in both of these examples it is engagement with the very activity of planting a seed – planning, soaking, digging, watering, observing – that lends itself to the cultivation of the spiritual life. Rather than performing rituals as prescribed by tradition or text, it is the life of the seed itself that intrinsically lends meaning to the observant.

Seeds as vehicles for connecting people with God and Earth

In the early 1990s, the Sisters of Providence of St. Vincent de Paul in Kingston, Ontario began a communal visioning process around what could be done with the 30 acres of land on which the convent sits in the midst of the city. Given that one of the religious community's values centers on ecological concerns, the sisters concluded that it would make sense to start a garden. Years prior to the visioning process, there had been an orchard, a garden, and a horse pasture on the land so it made sense to reclaim this part of the sisters' heritage. There was also strong interest to begin to gain more control over the food that the community ate, as well as to build a deeper relationship with the Earth. "We were trying to promote our rediscovery of our spiritual relationship with each and the earth," as Sister Jeannette Filthaut put it.[9]

Today the convent's property is home to a large organic garden which provides food for the sisters and for a local food bank and soup kitchen, a greenhouse for starting seedlings, and a 100-year-old restored barn that has been converted into an heirloom seed sanctuary. There the sisters dry and save hundreds of seed varieties and hold educational organic gardening workshops, including the popular "Seedy Saturdays" where participants can learn about seed saving and swap heirloom varieties. In March of 2016, Seedy Saturday hosted over 600 local area residents. Part of the program includes a "Meet the Seeds" session that catalogues the vast variety of seeds that the sisters grow on a rotating basis. Every seed variety is listed by cultivator name, botanical name, research date, and description. Listed are

73 varieties of beans, for instance, including a Black Knight (*Phaseolus coccineus*) that dates from 1654 and is a vigorous climber, red flowers, shell or dry, and black seed and a Hutterite (*Phaseolus vulgaris*) that dates from 1750 and is greenish yellow with dark hilum, oval, excellent in soups, and from the Hutterites (a religious sect from Austria) in western Canada.[10]

Central to the sisters' beliefs about the power of seeds is the idea that the material activities inherent to saving a diversity of heirloom or heritage seeds have a unique capacity for building rich and meaningful relationships between people and the land community to which we belong, with seeds, as integral members. "An heirloom seed is seed treasured by people who love the names, history, flavour, fragrance and feel of what plants share with them," the sisters say. "Saved seeds often become best friends, part of the family."[11]

Seeds as agents of social change

This theme runs in two directions: one of resistance to the injustices of the current industrial system of seed production, and one of promoting positive community-based change through seed planting activities. We return to Genesis Farm's involvement in the OSGATA v. Monsanto case as an example of how corporate produced transgenic seeds is understood as a form of oppression toward and injustice against small farmers. As Maine farmer Jim Gerritsen, president of the OSGATA states: "Our farmers want nothing to do with Monsanto. We are not customers of Monsanto. We don't want their seed. We don't want their gene-spliced technology. We don't want their trespass onto our farms. We don't want their contamination of our crops. We don't want to have to defend ourselves from aggressive assertions of patent infringement because Monsanto refuses to keep their pollution on their side of the fence. We want justice" (as cited in Marshall 2013). Conversely, seeds in this view are understood as vehicles for promoting positive community-based change. Farmer "D" Joffe puts it thus: "What greater metaphor for change is there than planting a seed? You water it, and before long, it grows. Over time it bears fruit. Finally, the wind and birds carry its seeds near and far, and more and more grows. Change in our communities is like that too" (Joffe 2014, 100). Suggestions for sowing seeds of change in community include planting herbs and vegetables in common areas to share, gardening where people can see you as a kind of public witness and educational tool, showing up at city hall to speak on behalf of community-based agricultural initiatives, and getting out in the community to volunteer at a local farm or nonprofit organization that is working to cultivate a garden.

Consider another example from Christian-based Eighth Day Farm in Holland, Michigan, whose work involves a "Backyard to Table" program in the neighborhood where the farm's founders, Jeff and Melissa Roessing and the seedling greenhouse resides. The "Backyard to Table" initiative focuses on building relationships with neighbors and educating around the gardening process. It works with residents to create backyard gardens from the ground up, helping to build raised beds, start and select seedlings from the neighborhood's greenhouse, put in and tend the garden, and cook with fruits and vegetables that may be unfamiliar. The program works to "address systemic food injustices including food insecurity by empowering households to grow their own food in backyard gardens and enabling them to recognize and demand better food."[12] In this way, seeds and their growth are practical tools of community empowerment and self-sufficiency, which Eighth Day understands as key to their mission and vision "to contribute to the restoration of the land and to the flourishing of communities so that all people have access to nutrient-dense food."[13]

To conclude: even as Jewish, Christian, and Muslim views of genetically modified seeds and food crops present no clear-cut response about its ethical permissibility, this is not to imply that anything goes in an Abrahamic food ethic. Rather, what it suggests is that there are rich and varied resources for considering the topic, making religious thought adept at developing context specific moral responses to an agricultural problem of global significance. What we will want to know is how attentive and agile religious communities can be in terms of engaging the issues as they arise, an organizational capacity that will be especially important in the face of shifting planetary circumstances. While the religious farms I spotlighted tend to be against the use of GM seeds, they nevertheless do so in community-based settings that are intended to provide a counterweight to the massive presence of large-scale corporate seed producers. In this way, they should be taken for what they are – faith as mustard seeds.

Notes

1 Along similar lines, philosopher, Paul Thompson notes in his *Food Biotechnology in Ethical Perspective* that the extant agricultural biotechnology literature categorizes five impact areas of the products and processes of rDNA: "(1) impact on human health (i.e. food safety); (2) impact on the environment; (3) impact on non-human animals; (4) impact on farming communities in the developed and developing world; and (5) shifting power relations (e.g. the rising importance of commercial interests and multinationals)" (Thompson 2007, 25).

2 See, for example, the Food and Faith blog of the Presbyterian Church (U.S.A.), www.presbyterianmission.org/food-faith/ (accessed October 15, 2017).

3 See Navdanya's website, www.navdanya.org/home (accessed November 29, 2016).

4 Ethical questioning over agbiotechnology and GM plants and animals have a much longer history in religious thought in relation to considerations of human genetic engineering that began to develop in the mid-1970s. As we shall see, much of that questioning is reflected in discussions about GM plants and animals, though some of it is not.

5 See the website Faith and GMOs for discussions by religious leaders of various faith traditions on the issue of GM foods: www.faithandgmos.org/ (accessed on February 20, 2014).

6 On the idea of lived religion, see, for example David Hall (1997), *Lived Religion In America: Toward A History Of Practice*, Princeton University Press, Princeton.

7 The lawsuit was filed by Public Patent Foundation (PUBPAT). For more on the issue see the PUBPAT webpage, "Organic Seed vs. Monsanto," www.pubpat.org/monsanto-seed-patents.htm (accessed October 2, 2017).

8 See the Hazon webpage, "Hazon Detroit: Seed Saving Workshop," https://hazon.org/calendar/hazon-detroit-seed-saving-workshop/ (accessed October 5, 2017).

9 See Sisters of Providence of St. Vincent de Paul website, www.providence.ca/our-work/heirloom-seed-sanctuary/ (accessed December 13, 2016).

10 Ibid, www.providence.ca/our-work/heirloom-seed-sanctuary/meet-the-seeds/

11 Sisters of Providence of St.Vincent de Paul website, accessed December 13, 2016 (www. providence.ca/our-work/heirloom-seed-sanctuary/).
12 See Eighth Day Farm website, www.eighthdayfarm.org/ (accessed December 15, 2016).
13 Eighth Day Farm website, www.eighthdayfarm.org/ (accessed December 15, 2016).

References

al-ayani, F.A. (2007) "Biomedical ethics: Muslim perspectives on genetic modification," *Zygon* 42:1, 153–162.

Allen Jr., J.L. (2009) "GMOs are going to create famine and hunger," *National Catholic Reporter* May 19, 2009. Interview with Sean McDonagh. Available at http://ncronline. org/news/ecology/gmos-are-going-create-famine-and-hunger (accessed on March 20, 2016).

Francis, Pope. (2015) *Laudato Si: On Care for Our Common Home*, Vatican Press, Rome.

Howard, P.(2009) "Visualizing consolidation in the global seed industry: 1996–2008," *Sustainability* 2009, 1, 1266–1287.

Joffe, D. (2014) *Citizen Farmers: The Biodynamic Way to Grow Healthy Food, Build Thriving Communities, and Give Back to the Earth*, Stewart, Tabori & Chang, New York, NY.

Marshall, L. (2013) "Genesis farm update: The case against transgenic seeds," January 2013. Available at http://genesisfarm.aetistry.com/system/res/17/original/Jan_2013_Seed_ Update_.pdf (accessed October 2, 2017).

Moosa, E. (2009) "Genetically modified foods and muslim ethics," in C.G. Brunk and H. Coward (eds.), *Acceptable Genes? Religious Traditions and Genetically Modified Foods*, SUNY Press, Albany, NY 135–158.

Omobowale, E.B., Singer, P.S., and Daar, A.S. (2009) "The three main monotheistic religions and gm food technology: An overview of perspectives," *BMC International Health and Human Rights* 9:18, 2009. Available at www.ncbi.nlm.nih.gov/pmc/articles/PMC2741 429/#B46 (accessed March 10, 2016).

Owen, R. (2003) "Vatican says GM food is a blessing," *The Times*, August 5, 2003. Available at www.agbioworld.org/biotech-info/religion/blessing.html (accessed March 2, 2016).

Parvaiz, M.A. (2003) "Scientific innovation and al-Mizan," R.C. Foltz, F.M. Denny, and Z. Baharuddin (eds.), *Islam and Ecology: A Bestowed Trust*, Harvard University Press, Cambridge, MA.

Shiva, V. (2003) "The war against farmers and the land," in N. Wirzba (ed.), *The Essential Agrarian Reader: The Future of Culture, Community, and the Land*, University of Kentucky Press, Lexington, KY, 121–139.

Shiva, V. (2000) *Stolen Harvest: The Hijacking of the Global Food Supply*, South End Press, Cambridge, MA.

Singer, P. and Mason, J. (2006) *The Ethics of What We Eat: Why Our Food Choices Matter*, Holzbrinck Publishers, New York, NY.

Thompson, P. (1997, 2007) *Food Biotechnology in Ethical Perspective*, 2nd edition, Springer Science & Business Media, Dordrecht.

Wilson, J. (2002) "Intellectual property rights in agricultural organisms:The shock of the not-so-new," in R. Ruse and D. Castle (eds.), *Genetically Modified Foods: Debating Biotechnology*, Prometheus Books, Amherst, MA, 151–62. Wirzba, N. (2011) *Food and Faith: A Theology of Eating*, Cambridge University Press, New York, NY.

Wolff, A. (2001) "Jewish perspectives on genetic engineering," October 2001. Available at www.jcpa.org/art/jep2.htm (accessed February 20, 2016).

Working Group on Genetic Engineering of the Justice, Peace and Creation Team (2005) "Caring for life: Genetics, agriculture and human life." Available at www.wcc-coe.org/wcc/what/jpc/geneticengineering.pdf (accessed March 25, 2016).

Zoloth, L. (2009) "'When you plow the field, your Torah is with you': Genetic modification and GM food in the Jewish tradition(s)," in C.G. Brunk and H. Coward (eds.), *Acceptable Genes? Religious Traditions and Genetically Modified Foods*, SUNY Press, Albany, NY, 81–114.

4

ANIMALS

Humane, sustainable, spiritual meat?

The problem of eating animals has preoccupied environmental ethicists since the field's inception in the 1970s. Early debates centered on the moral status of animals and on the value of individual sentient creatures in relation to species and ecosystems. Ecocentric thinkers such as Holmes Rolston III (1988), for example, argued that meat eating was part and parcel of ecological life and thus morally justifiable insofar as animals were treated humanely. Animal rights thinkers such as Peter Singer (1975) argued oppositely that meat eating was rationally indefensible and represented a particularly pernicious form of anthropocentrism and human domination of nonhuman animals. Some thinkers such as J. Baird Callicott (1980) attempted to bridge such seemingly irresolvable debates, proposing that holistic and animal rights views could be understood as a triangular, rather than an oppositional, affair. Since then, discussions related to meat eating and animal rights and welfare have been stretched to consider issues beyond axiological concerns. Now on the table are problems related to the welfare of food workers, deforestation, water use, quality, and scarcity, climate change, small versus large-scale animal agriculture, and industry and governmental standards.

Still, as philosopher Paul Thompson noted at the 2016 European Society for Agricultural and Food Ethics (EURSafe) annual conference, animal ethicists, particularly in the United States, have neglected to consider what a humane and sustainable animal production process might look like, taking the position that raising and harvesting animals for consumption is intrinsically unethical, and that, in turn, vegetarianism or veganism is the only viable option. Such neglect, I want to argue in this chapter, is too bad, for it disallows agricultural and food ethicists from engaging in meaningful discussions around the reality that most of the industrialized world eats meat. Add to that the fact that global meat production is projected to double by the year 2050. Moreover, meat eating is generally viewed as theologically and ethically permissible in Abrahamic faith traditions, making the problem of animal agriculture that much more relevant, particularly for this book's purposes, as an environmental topic worthy of critical consideration. What I am therefore most interested in exploring in this chapter are some of what I view as the more novel and nuanced "takes" on meat eating put forward by Christian, Jewish, and Muslim thinkers, especially in terms of how they interpret meat-eating's environmental dimensions. Highlighting such approaches helps to illuminate how some religious individuals and groups in the climate change generation are conceptualizing what food writer, Michael Pollan popularly termed "the perfect meal." For if meat is still on the table, we will want to know more about how it is being justified and according to which reasons.

To be clear, this chapter should in no way be read as a license to continue eating meat as we currently do. Quite the opposite, the authors and farmers it cites argue strongly that animal production and consumption can be viewed as defensible only insofar as certain environmental and religious principles are enacted. In this way, their claims buck conventional cultural norms of meat eating for how they fundamentally question dominant forms of large-scale animal agriculture. While the alternatives they present provide no magic bullet or comprehensive solution for addressing the gross mistreatment of people, animals, and land that goes on in much of the global livestock industry, they nonetheless provide clues, in a variety of directions, for how one might think more critically and intentionally about eating meat today.

What's the problem with beef for dinner?

Before we move on to examine the proposals of some contemporary Jewish, Christian, and Muslim authors who advocate for a more just and sustainable approach to meat eating, it is important to underscore some of the ecological costs associated with the global animal production system. The interlocking logics of animal and human abuse in current animal production practices are revealed as the chapter continues, but for now, given this book's focus, let us focus on meat eating's environmental costs. The Food and Agriculture Organization of the United Nation (FAO) United Nation's report, *Livestock's Long Shadow: Environmental Issues and Option* (Steinfeld 2006) cites four key areas of ecological concern when it comes to global animal production – land degradation, atmosphere and climate, water, and biodiversity. First, in terms of land use, livestock pasture uses over a quarter of the total ice-free land surface of the planet.[1] When land used for feedstock production is added, that figure jumps to 70 percent of total agricultural land use and 30 percent of the total land surface of the planet. The ongoing conversion of land from wild ecosystems to agriculturalized ones for the purposes of animal grazing and feed production has come to be referred to as the global "land grab." This is particularly prevalent in Latin America where approximately three quarters of formerly forested land in the Amazon has been converted to pasture for livestock, with feed crops occupying much of the remainder. Cattle production, with exports largely going to the European Union, is responsible for nearly 80 percent of deforested land in the Amazon. Other ecosystems that are particularly susceptible to land degradation when converted to animal production usage are rangelands in dry areas, where grazing leads to soil compaction and erosion, which in turn releases carbon that the soil would have naturally stored into the atmosphere.

Second, the livestock sector accounts for nearly 20 percent of the global warming effect, a higher percentage than the transportation sector. Even as the animal production process contributes one-tenth of anthropogenic *carbon* emissions, it emits significant percentages of more harmful warming gases, including 37 percent of anthropogenic methane (23 times the global warming potential (GWP) of carbon dioxide), 65 percent of nitrous oxide (296 times the GWP), and 64 percent of ammonia (which contributes to acid rain). Methane results from the process of enteric fermentation by ruminant animals such as cattle where through the digestion process gas from animals is literally belched out, and to a lesser extent passed as flatulence. Animal manure and urine are responsible for the production of nitrous oxide and ammonia in the atmosphere. Land conversion is among the most significant contributors of carbon emissions in the livestock sector since it involves the destruction of ecosystems such as forests that had formerly functioned as natural carbon "sinks" or sequesters of carbon in the atmosphere.

In addition, the livestock sector relies on planet warming fossil fuels to produce synthetic fertilizer, irrigate crops, and run machinery for animal feed. In the United States and Canada, half of synthetic fertilizer is used for feed crop production. Concentrated Animal Feeding Operations (CAFOs) – defined by the Environmental Protection Agency (EPA) as "facilities that confine animals for at least forty-five days a year and do not produce their own feed" – may hold more than 1,000 cattle, 2,500 hogs, and 125,000 poultry. What makes CAFOs so climate costly is the scale and type of feed used. Livestock in CAFOs do not pasture or eat things they would normally eat. From birth, they are fed a steady diet of corn, soybeans, and other foodstuffs, such as fishmeal. Ninety percent of all soy and half of all corn – one third of the globe's cereal harvest – is used to feed animals on industrial farms. In the United States alone, two-thirds of corn and 80 percent of soy goes not to feeding people, but to feeding animals. Of this, 19 percent is exported with much of this going to feed livestock in other parts of the world.

Third, over 80 percent of total global water use goes toward livestock production. At the same time, 64 percent of the world's population is predicted to live in water-stressed regions by the year 2025. The livestock sector, compared to any other, is likely responsible for the largest amount of total global water pollution as manure runoff, chemical fertilizers and pesticides for feedstock, antibiotics to expedite animal size and treat disease, and sediments from eroded pastureland leach into groundwater, waterways, lakes, and oceans. Such has contributed to the formation of "dead" zones in coastal waters, where accumulated toxins deplete the water's oxygen and in turn degrade and destroy plant and animal life in areas with radiuses that can stretch thousands of miles. The largest toxic dead zone in the United States, found at the mouth of the Mississippi River at the Gulf of Mexico, averages 5,700 square miles, which is larger than the state of Connecticut.

Fourth, in terms of biodiversity, livestock make up 88 percent, by volume, of all wild and domesticated animals combined, with the 30 percent of the planet's landmass that livestock currently occupy previously functioning as habitat for wildlife. Moreover, the byproducts of animal and feed production degrade aquatic and terrestrial ecosystems and undermine biodiversity. For these reasons, *Livestock's Long Shadow* concludes, "the livestock sector may well be the leading player in the reduction of biodiversity, since it is the major driver of deforestation, as well as one of the leading divers of land degradation, pollution, climate change, overfishing, sedimentation of coastal areas and facilitation of invasions by alien species" (Steinfeld 2006).

Based on livestock production's stark ecological impacts, it is not difficult to see why many environmental ethicists are fundamentally opposed to meat eating. Knowing this, how then have thinkers and practitioners within the Abrahamic traditions justified the practice?

Humane, sustainable, spiritual meat?

Especially in the past decade, the academic study of religion and theology has witnessed a surge of interest in the topic of animals. This follows a more general trend to include "animal studies" in a variety of disciplines from sociology to psychology to literature to political science. Religion scholars who study animals have taken a variety of approaches, including historical, comparative, theological, and ethical ones. For example, Lisa Kemmerer's *Animals and World Religions* (2012) and Paul Waldau and Kimberley Patton's *A Communion of Subjects: Animals in Religion, Science, and Ethics* (2006) present a plurality of global religious and secular worldviews on nonhuman animals and the human relationship to them. Recent theological and ethical treatments within the Abrahamic traditions include Aaron Gross' *The Question of the Animal and Religion: Theoretical Stakes, Practical Implications* (2015), David L. Clough's *On Animals* (2012), Laura Hobgood Oster's *The Friends We Keep: Unleashing Christianity's Compassion for Animals* (2010), Andrew Linzey's *Why Animal Suffering Matters: Philosophy, Theology, and Practical Ethics* (2009), Sarra Tlili's *Animals in the Qur'an* (2012), and Richard Foltz' *Animals in Islamic Tradition and Muslim Cultures* (2006). Despite such surge of interest, few religious treatments of animals have explicitly considered the topic meat eating in relation to the problems of industrial agriculture and environmental degradation. There have nonetheless been a handful of exceptions, and we examine them here.

Aaron Gross' humane subject

More than any other contemporary religion scholar, Aaron Gross has examined the problem of factory farming in the United States in the context of kosher slaughterhouses and Jewish perspectives on animals. Gross' 2015 book *The Question of the Animal and Religion* was born out of his academic reaction as a historian of religions and his personal reaction as a Jewish individual to a 2004 video he was mailed by a group of animal rights advocates. The video documented animal abuses at AgriProcessors, one of the world's largest religious slaughterhouses. Located in Postville, Iowa, a community of urban Hasidic Jews had moved to the historically Lutheran, rural town to run the slaughterhouse, which at its peak provided up to 40 percent of kosher poultry and 60 percent of kosher beef in the United States. Discovered during an undercover investigation by People for the Ethical Treatment of Animals (PETA), the animal abuses at AgriProcessors were first made public in a November 30, 2004, *New York Times* online article, "Videotapes Show Grisly Scenes at Kosher Slaughterhouse," which ran the following day in print ("Video Cited in Calling Kosher Slaughter Inhumane").

The article detailed the video footage of workers "systematically cutting and partially removing the esophagi and tracheas of cattle after *shechitah* – the biblical word for slaughter used today to designate the cutting of the animal's neck required by kosher law – but, in more than one out of every five slaughters, before the animals lost consciousness" (Gross 2015, 2). In one documented incident, a conscious cow lay writhing in its own blood in the corner of the slaughterhouse floor, esophagi and trachea hanging out, as workers continued to slaughter other animals until the animal in the corner was finally hoisted by mechanical hook to the next phase of the process. In 2008, additional investigations revealed that AgriProcessors had also been committing human rights abuses, both against undocumented immigrant workers, mostly Guatemalans, and underage workers, including 13- and 14-year-olds. Such prompted then Senator Barack Obama to state: "When you read about a meatpacking plant hiring 13-year-olds, 14-year-olds – that is some of the most dangerous, difficult work there is … They have kids in there wielding buzz saws and cleavers? It's ridiculous" (as cited in Gross 2015, 5).

Using the AgriProcessors case as a backdrop, Gross theorizes about the role of animals in the history of the study of religion by examining some of the field's major figures, including Emile Durkheim (1858–1917), Mircea Eliade (1907–1986), and Jacques Derrida (1930–2004). Gross uses this lens to interpret the human (particularly Jewish) relationship to food animals and meat eating, or, what he calls "sacrificing animals and being a mensch." "It is not that kosher practitioners – or anyone eating animals – first form a view of the world around them and then begins to eat in a certain way in response to it," writes Gross (Gross 2015, 148). "Before we eat animals, we are already, as the (Jewish) novelist Jonathan Safran Foer has expressed it, 'eating animals' – that is, we are animals defined in part by how we eat" (as cited in Gross 2015, 148–49). How we eat, meat eating or not, Jewish and otherwise, should be viewed through the frame of what Gross calls "the humane subject." The humane subject for Gross is not a normative ideal that applies in all circumstances, rather it is "a tool, a rubric, an analytic, and a methodology for making sense of the complicated ways in which animals in general, and in particular, animals that are eaten, are pressed into service of creating human subjects of a particular kind" (151).

Taking clues from Derrida's dialectical notion of the "sacrifice of sacrifice," Gross suggests two principles that are inextricably interwoven and in tension in the human relationship to animals: *ascendancy* and *kindness*. Ascendancy for Gross represents what Derrida refers to as the sacrificial quality of animal consumption whereby humans are in some sense dominionistic over animals. Gross states that he chose the term ascendancy for how it connotes the metaphor of height, a theme that runs through Jewish tradition in terms of the elevation of humans above animals in the order of creation. Kindness represents the anti-sacrificial pole, dually representing the ideas of similarity of kind between humans and animals and proper human attention to and concern for animals.

Gross goes on to explicate his humane subjects framework by examining key texts within the Jewish tradition, including the creation stories in Genesis 1 and 9, the writings of medieval thinkers Rashi (Shlomo Yitzhaki, 1040–1105) and Josheph Albo (1380–1444), the Talmudic story of Judah ha-Nasi's encounter with a calf being led to slaughter, and Rabbi Samuel Dresner's 1950's classic, *Keeping Kosher: A Diet for the Soul*. Gross concludes that these texts represent varying poles between the principles of ascendancy and kindness. The Priestly source of Genesis 1:26–30 equally represents ascendancy and kindness whereas Genesis 9:1–7 emphasizes ascendancy. Rashi and Albo focus on human ascendancy in interpreting the Genesis texts. The story of Judah ha-Nasi and the calf and the larger passage in which it is situated amplifies the idea of kindness in the humane subject typology. Dresner's *Diet for the Soul*, accentuates the principle of kindness, though specifically through the lens of kosher practice and what Dresner observes as an ancient lineage within Judaism of reverence for life.

Taken together, Gross argues that in the Jewish tradition one can read a "reverence for life ethic" and a "dominionistic ethic." "Both 'ethics'," he writes, "are…constituted by a basic family resemblance between various instantiations of the humane subject: on the one hand, those that…trumpet human ascendancy (among other things), and, on the other, those that emphasize the kinship of life and the regard for life that this kinship demands (among other things) (175). Responses to the AgriProcessors case too represent both types of ethics. A reverence for life ethic is evident in rejoinders issued by leadership within the Conservative Judaism movement, such as the Rabbinical Assembly which stated that PETA's work provided a "welcome, though unfortunate service to the Jewish community" and that Agriprocessors "must answer to the Jewish community, and ultimately, to God" (178). Even more radically, writes Gross, a reverence for life ethic can be seen in responses put forward by Jewish leaders such as Rabbi David Wolpe of Temple Sinai, one of the largest Conservative synagogues in the country, and writers such as Jonathan Safran Foer who advocate for a vegetarian diet (179). Conversely, Orthodox leaders who defended Agriprocessors kosher practices represent what Gross refers to as an even more extreme form of ascendancy, or, "a hyperdominionistic ethic." Such is seen in the response articulated by Haredi Orthodox rabbi, Avi Shafran, who stated that "the 'PETA Principle,' the moral equating of animals and humans, is an affront to the very essence of Jewish belief, which exalts the human being, alone among G-d's creations…That distinction is introduced in Genesis, where the first man is commanded to 'rule over' the animal world" (as cited in Gross 2015, 183).

Without being prescriptive, Gross concludes that vegetarianism and meat eating – along with critiques and defenses of industrial kosher meat production such as the one in the Agriprocessors case – represent distinct visions of humanity, ethics, and "of the kind of being Jewish tradition asks Jews to be" (193). Even as Gross' study overlooks important ecological considerations, both in terms of people's relationship to the land and the health of the land community itself, it nevertheless provides a helpful ethical framework for analyzing animal production and consumption practices on a continuum, an approach that has been sorely neglected in the study of environmental and food ethics and is resonant with this book's approach.

Norman Wirzba's agrarian meat eating

Similar to animal rights theologian and Anglican priest Andrew Linzey, Norman Wirzba draws, on the trinitarian stream of the Christian tradition to understand the activity of eating. Trinitarian thought stems from the work of the second century church father, Tertullian, who coined the Latin term *trinitas* (trinity) to refer to the interrelationship among Christianity's divine figures – God, Jesus, and the Holy Spirit. Different from Linzey's strong objection to the eating of animals along deontological lines, Wirzba emphasizes trinitarian thought's susceptibility to an evolutionary ecological reading of the human relationship to other organisms. Wirzba begins with the theological and ecological idea of death: "For us to live (and eat) well, we need to know what death is" (Wirzba 2011, 111). For Christians, he believes, this is "something which can only be known properly from within a Trinitarian perspective" (111). Wirzba quotes Swiss theologian and Catholic priest Hans Urs von Balthasar's (1905–1988) notion that death in the trinitarian theological view involves a transvaluative dimension. According to this view "it is a mistake to view all death as evil," writes Wirzba (111). There is, in other words, a good kind of death, one that becomes positive or beneficial in some sense, and an evil kind of death, one that serves no higher or better purpose. "Good death," as Wirzba interprets it, is a "kenotic passage through which life moves" (111).

Wizba observes that sacrificial ritual practices have historically helped people and communities make sense and meaning out of the intrinsically difficult elements of the experience of death, therefore rendering its transvaluative element. In the Hebrew bible, sacrifice "was fundamentally about entering into and nurturing a relationship with God," states Wirzba (119). On this idea, he quotes Jewish scholar, Jacob Milgrom: "In essence, the system of sacrifice provided a metaphor, a method, for the Israelites to reach God, responding to the deep psychological, emotional, and religious needs of the people. Indeed, this is the meaning of the Hebrew word for 'sacrifice'; it comes from a verb meaning 'to bring near.' Thus, a sacrifice is that kind of an offering that enables us to approach God" (as cited in Wirzba 2011, 119). The act of offering is important to the human–divine relationship because to "offer food to another expresses a profound insight in the gifted and interdependent character of the human condition. In this offering people acknowledge that as creatures they are beneficiaries of an incomprehensible and costly generosity and hospitality" (121).

Christian sacrificial practice is commonly understood as the spiritualization of Jewish rituals as animals were no longer used in altar sacrifice. Alternatively, early Christian sacrificial practice, notes Wirzba, focused upon the material practices of showing mercy and charity to the poor. "At the Eucharistic table, in the sharing of bread and wine and in the participation in the life and death of Jesus," writes Wirzba, "Christians see, smell, touch, and taste that life and love are possible because of the giving of life for each other" (129–30). Quoting Ghislain Lafont's *Eucharist: The Meal and the Word*, Wirzba concludes: "If, then, life is given us, we understand that it is by means of death. And if we in turn are to give life, death must likewise intervene" (as cited in Wirzba 2011, 130).

But what does all of this mean for a Christian view of meat eating? Wizba offers several suggestions. First, he states that no type of eating – vegan or vegetarian – can avoid inflicting death and the concerns that are inherent to the idea of sacrifice. Clearly, though, not all forms of death are equal, Wirzba recognizes. Moreover, vegetarians are so for various reasons, he notes, including those that relate to human health, animal welfare, and ecological sustainability. Despite these seemingly good reasons, Wirzba asks: Does it follow, however, that all consumption of meat is wrong? Are there theological considerations that can be brought to bear upon this very complex and important issue?

Wirzba acknowledges the conflicting views of eating animals that appear in the bible. On the one hand, the story of the Garden of Eden and later texts in the Hebrew prophets such as in Isaiah suggest that a vegetarian diet characterizes God's original paradise and future peaceable kingdom. On the other hand, Jesus did not explicitly address the issue of meat eating and Peter and Paul (Acts 10:9–16, Rom. 14) admonish that all animals are clean and fit to be eaten and that Roman church members should not judge one another based on whether they ate animals. Given the biblical ambivalence on the issue, Wirzba returns to the Christian theological ideal of sacrificial self-giving and offering: "Creation itself, understood as the physical manifestation of God's self-giving love, is the altar upon which this unfathomable grace is daily worked out. Creatures eat, grow, heal, and die as the expression of this sacrificial movement" (133). A refusal to eat meat, posits Wirzba "*may* reflect a refusal to come to terms with the life and death that characterizes creation. It *may* signal an inability to appreciate appropriate death as a movement into and constitutive of life" (133).

When creation is viewed as the material embodiment of God's sacrificial love, Wirzba writes, it is necessary that the production and eating of food acknowledges and respects the gift that it entails. Such implies that the food production and consumption process and the animals and land involved are treated with kindness and attentiveness toward their flourishing and health. So too it will mean that culturally the activities of raising and caring for animals in particular and agrarian acts more generally are seen as among society's most virtuous vocations. Animals can be eaten, in other words, "in ways that respect their integrity and well-being and that honor God. But for this condition be met it is crucial that these animals be accorded the attention and care that reflects God's own self-giving care for creation" (136–37).

Wirzba concludes with a short list of questions that a Christian "remembering of food" necessitates, each of which could be applied in an ethical assessment of meat eating. When deciding what to eat, he suggests, Christians should ask:

- Does the food we are about to eat reflect production practices in alignment with Christ's desire that creatures be whole and well?
- Were food providers honored for their work?
- Were they able to work in creative ways that encouraged participation in God's creative ways with the world?
- Are the soil and water from which our plants grow healthy and clean?
- Are biological rhythms and ecological integrity observed?
- Were the animals respected and treated with care?
- Is the food eaten distributed in an equitable manner?
- Does the eating we enjoy deprive others of the ability to eat well?
- Is food being grown and distributed in a way reflective of God's desire that all be fed? (201).

Wirzba's Christian agrarian outlook raises the question of whether a truly ecologically sustainable form of meat eating is possible in today's global economy and food system, a point further accentuated when we recall Gross' critique of industrial slaughterhouses such as AgriProcessors. A fraction of people, on a small scale, may be able to practice such "good" or "ethical" meat eating according to the principles Wirzba lays out, but not many. Does this mean that Christians should simply forgo meat eating altogether, or at least commit to only eating animals that they know for certain have been raised in the ways Wirzba outlines? That is the tact of the final author we read, who, similar to Wirzba argues that it is morally permissible to eat animals only when they are raised and eaten in ways that abide by certain spiritual and ecological principles.

Ibrahim Abdul-Matin's green zabiha

Most Islamic environmentalists, observes religion scholar, Richard Foltz, have advocated against vegetarianism for how it contradicts Islam's view that meat eating and serving meat is respectively a sign of prosperity and hospitality.[2] Still, they have done so uncritically, in Foltz' estimation, overlooking key Muslim thinkers who have argued against conventional animal production and for the adoption of a vegetarian diet for moral reasons. Animal rights advocate, Basheer Ahmad Masri (1914–1993), an imam in the English mosque of Shah Jehan in Woking, for example, issued strong protest against what he called "the Westernized meat industry." In his 1987 volume, *Islamic Concern Animals* Masri writes:

> Most of such un-Islamic businesses are flourishing in the Islamic countries due to the ignorance of the consumer public. People do not know how the chickens are being reared and how they are being fed on chemical nutrients to fatten fast and to produce more and more eggs. Fowls and other food animals are no longer creatures of God they are numbers on their computers...If only the average, simple and God-fearing Muslim consumers of such food animals knew the gruesome details about the Westernized meat industry in

their own Islamic countries, they would become vegetarians rather than eat such sacrilegious meat.

(As cited in Foltz 2006, 93)

Even as Masri did not publically advocate for all Muslims to become vegetarians, he nevertheless believed that, "Some may decide that the products of intensive factory farms are not suitable, both from the religious and the health points of view, and seek more naturally produced eggs and meat; or give up eating meat altogether" (as cited in Foltz 2006, 92).

In his *Green Deen: What Islam Teaches about Protecting the Planet* (2010), popular author and policy advisor in the New York City Mayor's Office on sustainability, Ibrahim Abdul-Matin builds on Masri's work by engaging the meat eating/vegetarian debate in contemporary Muslim–American perspective. Fundamental to Abdul-Matin's view is the idea that "the Earth is a mosque, and everything in it is sacred" (Abdul-Matin 2010, 1). The word "deen," Abdul-Matin observes, is Arabic for religion, path, faith, or way, such that Islam is a deen, along with Judaism, Christianity, and other faiths, including secular forms of spirituality. A green deen, according to Abdul-Matin, "is the choice to practice the religion of Islam while affirming the integral relationship between faith and the environment, or better, the natural world, the universe, and all that is in it" (3).

Using environmental principles developed by Islamic scholar, Faraz Khan, Abdul-Matin suggests that green deen practices involve the following Muslim spiritual ideas:

- Understanding the Oneness of God and His creation (*tawhid*)
- Seeing signs of God (*ayat*) everywhere
- Being a steward (*khalifah*) of the Earth
- Honoring the covenant, or trust, we have with God (*amana*) to be protectors of the planet
- Moving toward justice (*adl*)
- Living in balance with nature (*mizan*) (5).

Choices around food are at the core of enacting a green deen for Abdul-Matin. He attributes such a focus to his upbringing in a food conscious household, as well as his African, Cherokee, Arapahoe, Sioux ancestry, which included farmers and land-owners in Nebraska, upstate New York, and southern Virginia. He writes:

Thousands of years ago, Allah gave us the template for healthy eating: organic, free-range halal, or permissible, foods. By opting for locally grown seasonal produce and by using only meat from pasture-raised, grass-fed, and humanely treated livestock, we move away from the injustice of the factory farm system and toward practices that reflect the principle of justice (*adl*). We are what we eat, just as we are connected to everything in the universe because of the Oneness of God and His creation (*tawhid*).

(144)

Abdul-Matin catalogues the problems of inhumane animal treatment and land degradation associated with concentrated animal feeding operations (CAFOs), asking, "Is this how we want to treat the food that we will put into our bodies?" (148). Recognizing that millions of Muslims in the United States eat meat, Abdul-Matin argues that it is inevitable that they will have to either continue to rely on the current animal agriculture system, or create their own system to produce *halal* meat. The former choice is not promising, writes Abdul-Matin, particularly when one considers recent discoveries made in an investigation conducted by Mufti Shaykh Abdullah Nana and the Halal Advocates of America about the status of the halal industry and certification process. The investigation covered 35 slaughterhouses in the United States as well as those in the United Kingdom, Canada, and New Zealand that provide meat to U.S. markets. It found that there were routine violations of basic *halal* procedures, including "drive-by" blessings of slaughterhouses, the use of the same knife to process pork (forbidden in Islam and Judaism) and *halal* meat, and improper cuts to animals. Overall, Shaykh Abdullah Nana concluded that 50 percent of *halal* certified meat in America could not with certainty be called *halal* as specified in the *sunnah*, the teachings of Muhammad.

Similar to Wirzba's conclusions about meat eating, Abdul-Matin suggests that green Muslims might choose two paths to counteract industrial *halal* production: vegetarianism or organic, free-range *halal* meat. Abdul-Matin writes that it is possible to live an Islamic and environmentally oriented life and still eat meat. Abdul-Matin distinguishes between *halal*, *zabiha*, and *tayeb* meat in terms of its accordance with Islamic environmental principles. *Halal* meat is meat that has been slaughtered according to basic principles of a clean and humane cut to the animal so that the knife is uncontaminated by non-halal substances such as pork, wine, or shellfish, and that the animal does not suffer and bleeds out accordingly. *Zabiha* meat is meat that has been slaughtered in the same way, and is also accompanied by a pronouncement of Allah's name with the animal facing Mecca and a recitation of a Muslim blessing. *Tayeb* meat is meat where the animal is raised in a wholesome way, organically, naturally, happily, "the way God intended," according to Abdul-Matin. Reflecting on an experience he had had participating in a *zabiha*, *tayeb* Thanksgiving turkey slaughter with Yasir Syeed, founder of the organization, Green Zabiha, Abdul-Matin wrote:

> We slaughtered all sixty turkeys that day, and each time I participated, I felt like I was in a state of prayer. The slaughtering did not become rote. I imagined all the Muslims who would be ordering those turkeys for their Thanksgiving feasts, and it made me calm to think about how each bird had lived a good life, roaming free in the pasture and eating grass…There is an alternative to factory-farmed meat. The framework is simple: free-range, grass-fed, and blessed.
>
> *(177)*

Abdul-Matin recognizes that financial and cultural reasons often make it difficult for Muslims to eat this way. Organic meat is expensive and often not readily available.

So too, he writes, serving meat in Islam is a sign of prosperity and hospitality. If it were refused, for ecological or other reasons, it would tend to be viewed as a sign of ungratefulness and as a lack of appreciation for what is being offered. In Abdul-Matin's own life, he and his spouse have chosen to limit their meat eating. Where meat is offered that may not be free-range and organic, such as in their parents' homes, they eat small portions and use it as a time to engage in conversation about their food choices.

Abdul-Matin, along with Gross and Wirzba issue similarly strong critiques of large-scale industrial animal agriculture, and, in turn, offer alternative models that lean toward the small and local, marked by the virtues of care and concern for animals and for the health and flourishing of the land. Even as academic theologians and religion scholars have neglected to develop detailed practical alternatives to current forms of industrial animal agriculture, some religious communities and leaders have begun to enact these models on the ground along lines Gross, Wirzba, and Abdul-Matin suggest. In closing, I highlight two such examples.

Animal ministers: spiritual ecological models of meat eating

Ryan's Retreat

Located in Fort Plain, New York, a town with a population of just over 2,000 people approximately an hour's drive west of Albany, is Ryan's Retreat, a 20 acre farm run by parish pastor Nancy Ryan and her husband Will. Nancy is a minister in the Reformed Church in America (RCA), a mainline protestant denomination that originated in New York City (then New Amsterdam) in the early seventeenth century with the immigration of Dutch Calvinists to the United States. There are a significant number of RCA churches in the city, although there are even more in upstate New York and New Jersey where the Dutch eventually settled. Nancy has served as the pastor of Fort Plain Reformed Church since 1998. She and Will moved out to their farm and "began their adventure," as she calls it, roughly two years later. Nancy grew up on a hobby farm in upstate New York but did not know much about the nuts and bolts of farming until she and Will bought Ryan's Retreat. Will had initially stumbled upon the farm for sale on a wrong turn on the way back from a trip to the nearby town of Oneonta. Right from the start Will told me he loved the place. Set on a hill overlooking the valley, the expansive view mimicked the Atlantic Ocean feel of his upbringing on the Jersey Shore. They moved into what they now call Ryan's Retreat within a couple of months.

When I arrived at the farm for a tour in the summer of 2016, Nancy greeted me with a wave. She and Will were doing some sort of work outside of an old red barn with a field stone foundation that dated to a time prior to the civil war, as I would come to learn later over lunch. Will was working on a chicken coop inside the barn, so that the birds would not have free reign of the entire building as they had had since Nancy and Will added chickens to their farming operation. The first year that Nancy and Will were on the farm they kept some laying hens that the neighbor had brought over as a housewarming gift. With 20 acres of fields and woodlands they soon began thinking about cows and sheep. A local Amish farmer put in fencing. They got a couple of beef steer from a neighbor. The first year, Nancy told me, they brought the cattle to be butchered at 400 pounds and were sent home. "A waste of time and money at that weight," Nancy recalls the local slaughterhouse had told them. "We had no idea what we were doing." "We learned by asking people who knew what they were doing for help." "We had to exercise humility."[3]

Now the Ryan's farm is home to four cows, a dozen sheep and turkeys, two goats, fifty chickens, three dogs, and a host of predatory bird and wild animal species. Behind the house is a large garden that Nancy's 80-year-old mother, who lives with them, helps tend. Will tells the story of the first Thanksgiving they spent as a family on the farm. "Other than the cranberries and butter, everything on the table, we had raised or harvested." "That's a really good feeling," he said. "Much different than my Jersey upbringing."

Nancy emphasizes that their goal is not to make a profit, but to share with others what they have managed to produce over the years. They sell chickens and beef to family and friends and give away the surplus. Wine, she said, is another story since they did not want to get into licensing issues with the state. Instead, they barter the wine with their Amish fence-building neighbors – "hooch" as Nancy bemusedly says the Amish neighbors refer to it – and give away chickens and beef to a RCA camp and retreat center in the Adirondacks. By the end of the year, Nancy told me, they have an abundance of food and wine they basically need to get rid of.

I asked Nancy how she saw the intersection of her joint vocation as pastor and farmer. The farm is both retreat from and fodder for her ministry, she said. She gave an example from the previous summer where she had returned from a very emotionally straining church synod meeting, and had felt the farm's presence as a refuge: feeding animals, trimming fence line, and filling water were activities that replenish her, Nancy reflected. The everyday workings of the farm too have shaped her worldview and how she views her vocation as a minister, from birthing calves and ewes to cleaning turkeys and chickens to working with the land day in and out. Nancy says that she sees death in a different light, which has changed how she thinks about and performs the rituals of burial and funeral services. She says that she used to have a very hard time with these ceremonies. Through ongoing interaction with the life-death process on the farm, she said that she can now more readily grasp the goodness that emerges in the end. Still, it's hard, Nancy said, to kill the animals they raise. For this reason, they do not name the animals that they slaughter. The bull is Abraham and the mama cows, Pearly and Madame MaMa but the calf they will eventually slaughter they call "baby." The various animals that she has become attached to over the years have been allowed to live their lives out on the farm.

Echoing Gross's, Wirzba's, and Abdul-Matin's accounts, there is deep kindness, compassion, and care shown toward the animals at Ryan's Retreat. So too there is the kind of agrarian concern for the health and flourishing of land and human communities that Wirzba and Abdul-Matin emphasize. Add to that a pronounced self-reflective awareness about the ambivalence intrinsic to earthly life that is born out of experience on the farm and in turn integrated into religious life, and one can see emerging a model for thinking about the significance of farmer ministers such as Pastor Ryan in the food and faith movement.

Norwich Meadows Farm

Norwich Meadows Farm is a certified organic, community supported agriculture (CSA) farm located in upstate New York in the village of Norwich, approximately 450 miles north of New York City and an hour and a half south of Ryan's Retreat. Founded in 1998 by husband and wife team, Zaid and Haifa Kurdieh, the farm originally started as a half-acre back yard garden, with the Kurdieh's selling their fruits and vegetables locally. In 2000, they expanded their operation and incorporated as a CSA venture. Today, Norwich Meadows farms 80 acres of fruits and vegetables in Norwich and 20 acres of pastureland for their chickens in New Jersey.

During the growing season the Kurdieh's travel to New York City where they supply farmers markets and CSAs in Manhattan, Brooklyn, and the Bronx. They have also started a CSA in Norwich where local residents can pick-up weekly shares at the farm and volunteer in the greenhouses and with farming activities. Altogether, Norwich Meadows provides produce, poultry, and eggs to nine CSA's between New York City, Westchester County, and Norwich. Additionally, they sell their products to numerous local and regional restaurants, including Blue Hill, Good Egg, Gramercy, and Union Square Café.

The Kurdiehs, whose families historically originated and owned farmland in Palestine, are religiously observant Muslims and their farming and religious philosophies are inexorably intertwined. Zaid was trained in the agricultural sciences at the University of Wyoming and the University of South Dakota and worked after graduation training farmers for Cornell University's cooperative extension program. After Zaid and Haifa married and decided to start a farm of their own, they committed to using only organic methods, for the health of their own and other families and for the land. Now they are also concerned about the health and well-being of the chickens they raise. Their food philosophy reflects these ideals:

> We produce what we believe is good for our families and thus would be good for yours…We produce food that is free of harsh chemicals and is grown using natural fertilizers. Our chickens are free-running and are fed only the highest quality certified organic feed with a supplemental diet of organic greens. We strongly believe that food should nourish and not cause any harm to our bodies or the environment…
>
> For millions of years, the natural food system did not fail mankind. We not only survived, but flourished to a point of overpopulation. It is only within the past 100 years of man's brief time on earth that we have resorted to artificial and toxic means to grow our foods. As a result, we not only have

harmed our health, but we have dealt a blow to the very environment that supports our well-being.

No longer is there a lake, river or stream that is not contaminated with toxic agricultural chemicals. No longer is there a person who does not know someone who has cancer, or who has had a heart attack. There is only one way to reverse this destructive path and we believe we have taken the first and most important step and that was the decision to dedicate our god-given energies to the task of growing food as it was created, and to provide access to the local community for the betterment of its physical and economic health.[4]

Norwich Meadows practices the Islamic principles of *halal* and *tayeb*, which recall from Abdul-Matin, translate as permissible or fit and good or pure respectively. For Zaid, *halal* is not enough, rather, the food eaten must also be produced and harvested in a wholesome manner (*tayeb*) which means for Zaid that it is organic and treats farm workers fairly. This extends to the poultry production process at Norwich Meadows, which since 2006 has involved raising free-range chickens for eggs and meat. Prior to this, Zaid and Haifa had raised and slaughtered their own chickens for their family in order to be certain that they were raised in a way that was both *halal* and *tayeb*. "The Prophet gave animals certain rights," Zaid said in an interview for the popular food magazine, *Gastronomica*.[5] "That's why for the last fifteen years we haven't eaten any meat that we haven't slaughtered."[6] Now, they still raise and slaughter the animals themselves, but they do so for customers as well.

In addition to the *halal* poultry production, Norwich Meadows has created what they call a *halal* farm space, where Islamic dietary laws and holiday observances are practiced. In order to ensure this, the Kurdieh's have committed to hiring only Muslim farm workers who abstain from alcohol, which is forbidden in Islamic dietary laws, and who observe Muslim customs and holidays such as Ramadan. Doing so has been a challenge, they admit, as the pool of Muslim–American farm workers is not large. Hence, since 2007 Zaid has gone to Egypt to recruit farm employees, which presents its own challenges in terms of the extensive paper work that is required, as well as the psychological and cultural difficulties these workers often face when they come to the United States. Norwich Meadows Farm has also sought to hire Egyptian university graduates with agricultural degrees with the hope that the principles of sustainable and humane farming will eventually be introduced in the Middle East. "The Muslim world used to be self-sufficient," says Zaid "and it's not anymore. That concerns me."[7]

Note how in both cases Norwich Meadows' and Ryan's Retreat's farm work engages the broader communities and food systems in which they are embedded, despite their explicitly religious orientation. As the Kurdieh's put it, "We are just a small part of a much larger process and we realize we cannot achieve our goals alone. We need the support of a larger community. We invite all those who believe they can aid in our endeavor to join us."[8] Religious farms such as Norwich Meadows and Ryan's Retreat are significant for how they blur sacred and secular bounds in developing models of agricultural production that are understood to benefit the public good of developing healthier, more sustainable, and just food systems. In this book's final chapter, we examine more explicitly the sacred/secular dynamic in the context of religious farm sites. For now, we turn to another environmental issue taken up by religious traditions and communities engaged in food and farming work: water.

Notes

1 For the discussion that follows I am indebted to chapter 1 of Anna Lappé's *Diet for a Hot Planet: The Climate Crisis at the End of Your Fork* (2010, 3–41).
2 For arguments against vegetarianism in Islamic thought, see Foltz' *Animals in Islamic Tradition* (2006, 107–110). Foltz also notes: "The overwhelming majority of Muslims eat meat; indeed, meat-eating is mentioned in the Qur'an as one of the pleasures of heaven" (Foltz 2006, 25). Still, Foltz argues that a theological rationale for vegetarianism can be justified in Islamic tradition.
3 Personal communication, July 19, 2016.
4 Norwich Meadows Farm website, www.norwichmeadowsfarm.com/index.htm (accessed November 6, 2016).
5 Leah Koenig, "Reaping the Faith," *Gastronomica: The Journal of Food and Culture*, vol. 8, no. 1 (2007), pp. 80–84.
6 Ibid.
7 Ibid.
8 Norwich Meadows Farm website, www.norwichmeadowsfarm.com/index.htm (accessed November 9, 2016).

References

Abdul-Matin, I. (2010) *Green Deen: What Islam Teaches about Protecting the Planet*, Berret-Koehler Publishers, San Francisco, CA.
Callicott, J. B. (1980) "Animal liberation: A triangular affair," *Environmental Ethics* 2:4, 311–338.
Clough, D.L. (2012) *On Animals, Vol. 1: Systematic Theology*, Bloomsbury Publishing, New York, NY.
Foltz, R.C. (2006) *Animals in Islamic Tradition* and *Muslim Cultures*, Oneworld Publications, Oxford.
Gross, A. (2015) *The Question of the Animal and Religion: Theoretical Stakes, Practical Implications*, Columbia University Press, New York, NY.
Kemmerer, L. (2012) *Animals and World Religions*, Oxford University Press, New York, NY.
Koenig, L. (2007) "Reaping the faith," *Gastronomica: The Journal of Food and Culture*, vol. 8, no. 1, pp. 80–84.
Lappé, A. (2010) *Diet for a Hot Planet: The Climate Crisis at the End of Your Fork*, Bloomsbury USA, New York, NY.
Linzey, A. (2009) *Why Animal Suffering Matters: Philosophy, Theology, and Practical Ethics*, Oxford University Press, Oxford.
Oster, L.H. (2010) *The Friends We Keep: Unleashing Christianity's Compassion for Animals*, Baylor University Press, Waco, TX.
Pollan, M. (2006) *The Omnivore's Dilemma: A Natural History of Four Meals*, Penguin Press, New York, NY.
Rolston, H. (1988) *Environmental Ethics: Duties to and Values in the Natural World*, Temple University Press, Philadelphia, PA.
Singer, P. (1975) *Animal Liberation*, New York Review, New York, NY.

Steinfeld, H., Gerber, P., Wassenaar, T., Castel, V., Rosales, M., and de Haan, C (2006) *Livestock's long shadow: Environmental Issues and Options*, Food and Agriculture Organization of the United Nations, Rome.

Tlili, S. (2012) *Animals in the Qur'an*, Cambridge University Press, Cambridge.

Waldau, P. and Patton, K. (eds.) (2006) *A Communion of Subjects: Animals in Religion, Science, and Ethics*, Columbia University Press, New York, NY.

Wirzba, N. (2011) *Food and Faith: A Theology of Eating*, Cambridge University Press, New York, NY.

5

WATER

Precious, polluted, purified

The agriculture–water nexus is as tightly bound as the agriculture–soil nexus, if not more so. Without water, there is no food. Without soil, one can still grow food (think aquaculture), but not so without water. Furthermore, current agricultural practices use a huge percentage – 70 percent on some accounts, over 90 percent on others – of the world's fresh water supply, more than any other human activity, making the water–agriculture issue even more significant as a contemporary environmental problem. And there's more: by 2050 it is projected that the agricultural demand for water will increase by an additional 19 percent.[1] Add to that the fact that food itself is intrinsically watery. The water used on fields, for milling, washing, feeding, cooling, packaging, and transporting all goes into producing our food. Every time we hold a piece of food, as religious ethicist, Christiana Peppard notes, we are in fact "holding a history of water." Lester Brown, coiner of the term *sustainable development*, puts it succinctly: "the water problem and the food problem are in large measure the same" (Brown 1997, 31).

Yet, as Brown also notes, "There is a tendency in public discourse to talk about the water problem and the food problem as though they are independent" (31). As a result of this, most of us, especially those of us living in the Global North, do not readily see the close connections between water and our food. One of the main purposes of this chapter, then, is to uncover and reveal just how closely linked is the agriculture–food–water nexus. Its other main task is to examine some of the ways in which Jewish, Christian, and Muslim groups are engaging the agriculture–water conundrum in their teachings and practices. For even as water is viewed as a sacred entity in each of these traditions, it appears from the extent of today's global water crisis that such views of sacred water are not currently being taken to heart.

When we run out, we run out

In her 2014 book, *Just Water: Theology, Ethics, and the Global Water Crisis*, Peppard distinguishes several types of water usage. Most of the time we talk about water use, Peppard notes, we are referring to fresh water withdrawals where water is diverted or taken from a particular source and then used for agricultural, industrial, or domestic purposes. Not all water withdrawals, however, are equal in terms of their environmental effects. Nonconsumptive withdrawals, on the one hand, return water to the watershed in ways that the water can be reused for other purposes. Consumptive withdrawals, on the other hand, permanently withdraw water from the watershed in ways that render the water no longer useable.

Agricultural water use is highly consumptive, especially when compared with other industrial and domestic forms of water use, which combined account for 30 percent of total water withdrawals and consume only about 10 percent of that. Agricultural water use accounts for 70 percent of fresh water withdrawals, and 90 percent of global water consumption. If total green (rain-fed) and blue water (liquid water from rivers and aquifers) are considered, agriculture accounts for 86 percent of all water use (Deutsch et al. 2010, 98). "In agriculture, little of the water withdrawn is returned to the system," observes Peppard (2014, 24). "Instead, it is transformed into fruits, grains, and other agricultural products...Because agriculture consumes more water than it returns, it contributes to the depletion of fresh water supply" (24).

> Water use in livestock production is particularly intensive. In animal production water is used for meeting animals' drinking needs, servicing (e.g., to wash and cool animals, clean production facilities, and dispose of wastes), processing livestock products (e.g., slaughter, tanning), and producing animals feeds. The annual global water requirements for the first three uses are estimated to be relatively small...less than 1% of total annual human freshwater withdrawals...producing a growing amount of feed for animal on the other hand, constitutes a very large freshwater use....in terms of freshwater use, the water flow needed to sustain plant growth for animal feed is by far the dominant freshwater resource challenge in the livestock sector, affecting both blue and green water flows in the hydrological cycle.
>
> *(Deutschet al. 2010, 98)*

So, where does all of the water used for agricultural purposes come from? For most of agricultural history, water came from seasonal cycles of precipitation or from natural sources or wells. The twentieth century, however, witnessed a massive proliferation of technological developments in water withdrawals, including large-scale dams, deep wells, irrigation canals, and hydraulic drilling, all of which have profoundly altered the world's hydrological systems (Peppard 2014, 25). Take the fact that most of today's agriculture is watered from groundwater (or blue water) in the forms of liquid rivers and aquifers. "Aquifers are underground geological formations that are natural holding areas for fresh water. They come in all sizes and are composed of a range of types of sediments" (Peppard 2014, 26). Groundwater for agricultural or other purposes is extracted through the use of hi-tech hydraulic pumps that then deliver it to farmers and municipalities through irrigation canals and piping networks. Advanced extractive technologies have dramatically increased the amount of fresh water that is globally available.

"The problem," writes Peppard "is that many aquifers do not recharge on any humanly meaningful scale. Most aquifers take upward of ten thousand years to refill...many aquifers take much, much longer to refill—on the order of millions of years" (26). Water of this magnitude is often referred to as "fossil water" and its extraction as "water mining." Consider the Ogallala Aquifer that runs under eight states in the Midwest:

> Sprawling beneath eight states and more than 100 million acres, the Ogallala Aquifer is the kind of hydrological behemoth that lends itself to rhapsody and hubris. Ancient, epic, apparently endless, it is the largest subterranean water supply in the country, with an estimated capacity of a million-billion gallons, providing nearly a third of all American groundwater irrigation. If the aquifer were somehow raised to the surface, it would cover a larger area than any freshwater lake on Earth – by a factor of five.
>
> *(As cited in Peppard 2014, 87)*

Since 1990, the water in the Ogallala has declined by nearly 100 feet due to hydraulic extraction. Robert Glennon, author of the popular 2002 book *Water Follies*, states that "excessive groundwater pumping has caused the ground to collapse; rivers, lakes, and springs to dry up; and riparian habitat to die. If we continue to exploit our groundwater resources in this way, we will eventually run out" (as cited in Peppard 2014, 86). Fresh water is *sui generis*, Peppard concludes. It is, in other words, "of its own kind." "No other substance will suffice to replace fresh water's life-mediating properties" (29). When we run out, we run out.

A river runs through it

The problem is not only that industrial agriculture *uses* so much fresh water, it is also that it *pollutes* it, rendering it unfit for crop and livestock uses, as well as for nourishing healthy ecosystems and habitat for people and the rest of the living world. Livestock production in particular is responsible for a large portion of the pollution of local water systems. As water expert Maude Barlow emphasizes in her 2013 book *Blue Future: Protecting Water for People and the Planet Forever*, much of water's degradation has to do with the increasing size and scale of livestock production worldwide. Recall that only a handful of global corporations control the majority of livestock production, which has steadily risen over the past decade and is projected to continue to rise with the expanding human population. Take the beef-packing industry, 83 percent of which is controlled by just four companies headed by the global corporations, Tyson and Cargill. Brazil's JBS, the world's largest beef producer, owns Five Rivers Cattle Feeding whose thirteen feedlots in the United States and Canada have the capacity to hold 980,000 cattle. The largest operation is located in Yuma, Colorado and houses 110,000 animals (Barlow 2013, 161).

Here is how Barlow describes the livestock production–waste–water problem – in this case in the hog production industry:

> The feces and urine produced by the hog farms of corporations such as Smithfield, the largest pork producer and packer in the world contain ammonia, methane, hydrogen sulphide, cyanide, phosphates, nitrates, heavy metals, antibiotics, and other drugs. They fall through catchment floors to lagoons below that can hold as much as 180 million litres of toxic waste water. North Carolina's 11 million hogs create massive amounts of sewage. In just one of these factories, 2,500 pigs produce 100 million litres of liquid waste, 4 million litres of sludge, and 44 million litres of slurry (water plus manure) per year. Over the past decade, many lagoons have spilled their toxic contents into local water ways, and hog waste is largely considered the culprit for a massive fish kill in the Neuse River in 2003.
>
> *(Barlow 2013, 161)*

And the problem does not end with production. The slaughtering process uses and pollutes a huge amount of localized water sources. The second largest slaughterhouse in the world operated by Smithfield in Tar Heel, North Carolina butchers up to 34,000 pigs a day. In the process of doing so, the facility uses eight million liters of water and dumps twelve million liters of waste water into the nearby Cape Fear River – every day (161–62).

Downstream or nonpoint pollution magnifies the problem when it comes to the agriculture-water issue. Even as the proliferation of petrochemical use since the Green Revolution has significantly increased crop yield, it has also adversely affected the biology of soils and contributed to the collapse of aquatic ecosystems worldwide. The United Nations Department of Economic and Social Affairs (UNDESA) concludes: "Globally the most prevalent water quality problem is eutrophication, a result of high-nutrient loads (mainly phosphorus and nitrogen [from agricultural runoff and animal waste]), which substantially impairs uses of water" (2015). Evidenced most dramatically in freshwater and ocean dead zones (scientifically termed "eutrophication-induced hypoxic areas"), some 95,000 square miles of water in 400 distinct ecosystems are now impacted.

Dead zones are caused by the nitrates, nitrites, and phosphorous found in agricultural fertilizers and animal waste, which then run-off into ditches and small streams and creeks that flow into larger rivers and eventually empty into the world's oceans and fresh water lakes. Once the nitrogen and phosphorous-based nutrients empty into a larger body of water they serve as a kind of super-starter for algae production, leading to the formation of "algal blooms." Eventually, the algae die and sink to the bottom of the ocean or lake floor where bacteria then feed on them, causing oxygen to be sucked out of the rest of the aquatic system. Examples of lakes with severe (toxic cyanobacterial) blooms include Lake Taihu in China, Lake Winnipeg in Canada, Lake Nieuwe Meer in The Netherlands, and Lake Erie in the United States (Michalak 2013).

The largest dead zone in the United States – some 5,700 square miles, which is larger than the state of Connecticut lies at the mouth of the Mississippi River in the Gulf of Mexico, where 1.7 million tons of nitrates, nitrites, and phosphorous a year run-off Midwestern farms. Executive director of the Louisiana Universities Marine Consortium, Nancy Rabalais likens the Gulf dead zone to "stretching a sheet of plastic wrap from the mouth of the Mississippi River west to Galveston, Texas, and sucking out all the air" (as cited in Greenberg 2013). In his 1974 book *The Algal Bowl*, freshwater scientist John R. Vallentyne predicted that by the year 2000 the eutrophication of the world's freshwater systems would be equivalent to the extreme land degradation that occurred during the Great American Dust Bowl. Some three decades later, Vallentyne with water scientist David Schindler published a second edition of the book (2008), concluding that the prediction had largely come true.

If there were a silver lining to the problem it would be this, writes journalist, Paul Greenberg: "there is something about dead zones that makes them different from many other seemingly intractable environmental crises: Dead zones can be fixed" (Greenberg 2013). Greenberg points to water researcher Laurence Mee's findings about the dead zone at the mouth of the Danube River in the Black Sea, which, in the 1990s was the world's largest. With the fall of the Iron Curtain, fertilizer subsidies to countries along the river dropped, resulting in a significant decrease in nitrogen and phosphorous run-off. Greenberg concludes: "Indeed, as the Danube/Black Sea system showed, the equation is simple: Turn off the flow of nutrients into rivers, and dead zones go away" (Greenberg 2013).

Technological innovation is certain to play a key role in the reduction of the use of petrochemical fertilizers and pesticides and the polluting agricultural runoff they cause. So too desalination of the world's salt waters will significantly contribute to abating the global water crisis, as already shown in places such as Qatar and southern California. Yet as Peppard rightly argues, even as "technology is and will continue to be an important component of global fresh water supply…it must be deployed within a more general ethical framework that involves straightforward objectives, rigorous social and environmental impact assessments, effective paradigms for implementation, and clear channels of accountability" (Peppard 2014, 31). We will need to ask, for example, "What are the potential downstream consequences? Who bears the burdens, and who benefits?" (30–31).

Burdens and benefits of agriculture's water problem

As environmental justice scholars and activists routinely point out, when it comes to the current environmental crisis, including the water and agricultural crisis, we are *not* all in this together. It is the most vulnerable and historically oppressed groups of people who are most significantly and negatively affected by the current planetary crisis. The issue of water is no exception. In fact, it may just provide the most acute example of global environmental injustice we have today.

Women and children are the most seriously impacted by the effects of water pollution and scarcity caused by current agricultural practices, for they spend the largest amount of time devoted to managing daily water-oriented activities. This is particularly true in the Global South where water collection often requires walking long distances, consuming a significant portion of a day's time. Additionally, women are oftentimes the ones responsible for farming activities, from tilling and planting fields to bringing goods to markets. The upshot of such realities is that the more polluted and scarce water becomes the greater the negative impact on women and children especially. International nonprofit organization, Water.org observes the following:

- In just one day, 200 million work hours are consumed by women collecting water for their families. This lost productivity is greater than the combined number of hours worked in a week by employees at Walmart, United Parcel Service, McDonald's, IBM, Target, and Kroger.
- Surveys from 45 developing countries show that women and children bear the primary responsibility for water collection in the vast majority (76%) of households. This is time not spent working at an income-generating job, caring for family members, or attending school.[2]

Conversely, those of us living in the Global North consume an exorbitant amount of water compared to those in the Global South. People living in sub-Saharan Africa, for example, use 10 to 20 liters of water per person a day, while Europeans use 200 liters a day and North Americans and the Japanese use a whopping 350 liters a day. Even a child born in the Global North consumes 30 to 50 times more water than a child born in the southern hemisphere (Barlow 2013, 12).

Yet as global income inequality continues to grow and water is increasingly converted to a market commodity, poverty, class, and race across hemispheres become increasingly significant factors in determining who has access to clean water and who does not. Such is evident in my home state of Michigan where, despite our water rich location in the Great Lakes basin, water crises have devastated predominantly African–American communities in Flint and Detroit. On the flip side, some of the poorest and most water scarce countries in the world have individuals who have plenty of fresh water at their disposal simply because they can pay for it. Barlow notes an example observed by Indian movie director, Shekhar Kapur:

> In Mumbai. Just across the road from Juhu Vile Parle Scheme, all the beautiful people and film stars live opposite a slum called Nehru Nagar. Once a day, or maybe even less, water arrives in tankers run by the local 'water mafia' and their goons. Women and children wait in line for a bucket of water, and fights break out as the tankers begin to run dry.

Yet literally across the road, the 'stars' after their workouts in the gym or a day on a film set can stay in the shower for hours. The water will not stop flowing. Often at less than half the cost that the slum dwellers pay for a single bucket of water.

(As cited in Barlow 2013, 13)

Privatizing (sacred) water

The real "winners," if we want to call them that, in the agriculturally generated water crisis are the corporations and investors that profit from buying and trading on the global water market. The conversion of water into an asset that can be bought and sold by private entities has been going on for decades, yet water's privatization has dramatically increased in the past ten years, such that today the world's major banks, including JP Morgan Chase, Goldman Sachs, Deutsche Bank, Barlays Bank, and Credit Suisse have investment funds focused specifically on water as a profitable asset (as cited in Barlow 2013, 76). Citibank's chief economist Willem Buiter has gone as far to say that water will "become eventually the single most important physical-commodity based asset class, dwarfing oil, copper, agricultural commodities and precious metals" (as cited in Barlow, 77). Global agribusinesses and foreign governments too are increasingly acquiring water rights through the purchase of large tracts of land. Since 2008, the World Bank estimates that some 45 million hectares have been "grabbed" by 62 different countries in 41 countries spanning every continent except Antarctica (Ahmad 2015b, 14).

Global development financial organizations such as The World Bank and the International Monetary Fund (IMF) play a substantial role in recent trends in the privatization of the world's fresh water for agricultural purposes. The Bank's economic policies focus heavily on the deregulation and privatization of developing countries' water sources, which means that large corporations that deal in water are among those that profit most from its loans. As Vandana Shiva (2002) notes, the World Bank's collaboration with global agbiotechnology giant Monsanto reaches as far back as the early 1990s. Shiva quotes Monsanto's 1991 "Sustainable Development Sector Strategy" which forecasts its potential investment involvement with the Bank:

> First we believe that discontinuities (either major policy changes of major trendline breaks in resource quality or quantity) are likely, particularly in the area of water, and we will be well positioned via these businesses to profit even more significantly when these discontinuities occur. Secondly, we are exploring the potential of non-conventional financing (non-governmental organisations, World Bank, USAID, etc.) that may lower our investment or provide local country business-building resources.

(As cited in Shiva 2002, 88)

Today, the World Bank is the world's largest multilateral financer of water projects in the Global South with a total of 35 billion dollars in investments.[3]

Shiva (2002) cites the well-known case of Cochabamba, Bolivia as an example of grassroots political resistance to the World Bank's water privatization policies. In 1999, the World Bank suggested that the Cochabamba municipal water company (Servicio Municipal del Agua Potable y Alcantarillado (SEMAPA) cede its control of the city's fresh water supply to International Water, a subsidiary of Bechtel Corporation, the U.S.'s largest construction and civil engineering firm. As a result, local residents' water bills increased immensely, to the point that the $20 dollar/month bill was the same amount needed to feed a family of five for two weeks. By January of 2000, La Coordinadora de Defensa del Agua y de la Vida (The Coalition in Defense of Water and Life) formed, organizing protests and strikes, including the shutdown of the city's transportation system.

"Water is Life" and "Water Is God's Gift" were ideas central to the protestors insistence that all people had the right to safe and clean water. In response to the protests, city officials initially promised to reduce water price hikes, yet in the end acted to silence protesters by inflicting arrests, killings, and the censorship of the media. The protestors prevailed, however, and on April 10, 2000, Cochabamba's water supply was turned back over to the people. Bechtel subsequently sued the Bolivian government for $50 million in damages and lost profits, though the charges were dropped in 2006. La Coordinadoora has worked hard to implement a public management and decision-making system based on principles of "water democracy," as Shiva (2002) notes, but it has not been easy in the face of ongoing global pressure to privatize.

Trading (sacred) water

Trading water rights is a particularly divisive type of privatization that has emerged in the past two decades. In this case, it is farmers and landowners who sell their land and water rights – and developers and residents from municipalities that purchase them – that benefit from the water transaction. Historically, water rights in the United States have belonged to those whose land contained or abutted a water source, so that water rights were inherited when land was passed down within a family or when the land was purchased or made claim to. This has been a particularly prevalent issue in the western United States where water rights have been awarded on a "first in time, first in right" basis. United States water rights laws have not in the past permitted landowners to transport water beyond the boundaries of the watershed where the water source is located. But today the practice of shipping water from one area to another for agricultural, municipal, or corporate uses has become commonplace. Some farmers, especially in drought-ridden places such as California and Colorado, are allowing their agricultural fields to go fallow so they can instead sell the water to developers and municipalities in other areas. Referred to as "buy and dry," farmers in some instances have proposed to sell their water rights to developers for upwards of tens of millions of dollars, such as was recently the case in California's San Joaquin Valley (Barlow 2013, 79).

In other instances, farmers and landowners sell their water rights to municipalities that then pipe the water to other cities that are oftentimes significant distances from the water's source. In one especially conflict-ridden case, farmers in Ault, Colorado were approached by an anonymous buyer that, unbeknownst to Ault residents, had been hired by the Denver suburban city of Thorton, some 60 miles outside of Ault. The buyer was successful in purchasing most of the farmland in and around Ault and having the land's status changed from agricultural to municipal use. In the state of Colorado once this change occurs it cannot be reversed, as Ault landowners only learned after the sale. Adding insult to injury, municipalities are not required to pay property tax, which meant that in Ault's case the tax base for funding local schools and infrastructure projects significantly decreased with the city of Thorton as the new landowner (Baker 2016). Residents of Ault took the city of Thorton to water court where it sat for 12 years. In the end, Thorton officials agreed to pay the city of Ault an annual fee in lieu of property taxes and plant native grasses on former cropland to avoid future dust storms. These measures, nevertheless, do not change the fact that the town's landscape, economy, farming heritage, and identity have been and will continue to be altered by the sale of its water, pointing again to just how tightly bound the water–(agri)culture connection is.

Restoring sacred water

In Judaism, Christianity, and Islam water is understood in sacred terms – as a gift from God, a miracle of creation, and a symbol of divine activity in the world. The Qur'an states that water is a sign of Allah's mercy and grace: "And have you seen the water that you drink? Is it you who brought it down from the clouds, or is it We who bring it down? If We willed, We could make it bitter, so why are you not grateful?" [Qur'an 56: 58–70] (Ahmad 2015a, 3). In the Hebrew bible, the watery primordial deep (Hebrew: *tehom*) is the life source of all creation, including the land, oceans, rivers, birds, and fish (Troster). Christianity views water as the central sign of rebirth and renewal where in the sacrament of baptism initiates are believed to share in the death and rising of Christ and in Jesus' own baptism in the Jordan River (Matthew 3, Mark 1, Luke 3) (Harper).

But how, if at all, have such sacred meanings for water been reinterpreted in light of the global realities of water pollution and commodification just noted? What happens, in other words, to water's sacredness when it becomes degraded, depleted, dried-up – profaned – as it has in so many instances today? Several types of religious responses are noteworthy.

First, some faith-based groups are drawing on *sacred texts and teachings* to spotlight the moral and spiritual significance of water's degradation. Take the interfaith environmental organization, GreenFaith, which has developed a program called Water Shield. Water Shield is a certificate provided for faith-based institutions that have taken steps, educational, spiritual, and practical, to conserve water, protect water quality, and mobilize its members and the broader community to do the same.[4] Part of the program includes religious education materials on teachings about water from a variety of spiritual traditions. Each tradition's study guide begins with a list detailing the following problems, including, notably, current agricultural practices:

> The world's supply of fresh water faces serious threats. As the world's population grows, water use increases, as does sewage-contaminated water, polluted agricultural runoff, and water contaminated from industrial, commercial and residential uses. Suburban sprawl is a global phenomenon, increasing polluted runoff from storm water and lacing aquifers with chemical residues.
>
> In addition, over 880 million people lack access to clean drinking water. In a growing number of locations, lack of access to fresh water creates political instability. This will only get worse. Weather pattern changes due to climate change, resulting in droughts in some parts of the world and floods in others, will create an estimated 250 million climate refugees by 2050. Always a source of life, water will also be a source of international insecurity.[5]

The guides also explain the historical significance of water for each faith tradition. So, for example, in Judaism's case, there is a focus on ancient Israel's sensitivity to the "ecology of the land" and specifically to rain, noting that biblical Hebrew has at least ten words for "rain" and eight for "cloud" given Israel's lack of major waterways compared to surrounding Mesopotamia and Egypt (Troster). The remainder of each guide presents key pertinent scriptural and theological beliefs on water. Again, with Judaism, the following themes are given:

Blessing and covenant, and final promise – In Jewish theology, abundant rain is an expression of divine blessing and approval, a means of measuring Israel's commitment to the covenant, and a matrix from which life emerges." Biblical texts that represent this idea come from Deuteronomy 11:10–17, a source for the second paragraph of the *Sh'ma* and Isaiah 12:3, chosen to begin the *Havdalah* ceremony: "Joyfully shall you draw water from the fountains of salvation."

Life-source and creation – "Water also plays a key role in the Hebrew Bible's various stories of the Creation." Biblical texts are drawn, for example, from Genesis 1, Psalm 104, Job 38:8–11 on God's interaction with the primordial waters and design for creation.

Wash me, clean me – Water played a central role in the water purification rituals of the ancient temple/tabernacle (Exodus 29, Leviticus 1–7, 12–15), the Rabbinic ritual bath of the *mikvah*, and the more recent water ritual of the *Tashlikh* (Micah 7:18–20).

Metaphor for divinity – "In the Hebrew Bible, water, wells, dew, rain, cisterns and fountains serve as metaphors for the divine, or divine attributes." Recurring biblical metaphors for God include "Fountain of Living Waters" (Hebrew: *mekor mayyim hayyim*), for wisdom "fountain of life" (Proverbs 18:4) and for justice (Amos) (Troster).

Each faith tradition's guide closes with several questions for further reflection, including: "How can purity laws be interpreted today in a way that supports water conservation and protection?" "What water metaphors work today?" "What is your water ethic?"

Second, consider religious responses that focus on the reinterpretation of *sacred rituals* in light of the current water crisis. Contemporary interpretations of the Muslim practice of *wudu* and of the observance of Ramadan, for example, underscore this type of approach. *Wudu* is the ritual ablution Muslims use to prepare for prayer (*salat*), whether at home or at the mosque. Some Muslim groups such as GreenFaith's Muslim GreenWorship effort work to encourage congregations and facilities to conserve water during *wudu* based on the teachings of Muhammad who is said to have "made *wudu* with less than one half a liter of water."[6]

A more explicitly agricultural example comes from Muslim communities that are working to develop environmental approaches for the observance of Ramadan, one of the five "pillars of Islam."[7] Ramadan is celebrated during the ninth month of the Islamic lunar calendar and lasts 29 to 30 days depending on the visibility of the crescent moon. Ramadan's central spiritual practices include daily prayer and fasting (for the able bodied) from just before sunrise to sunset. The evening meal where Muslims gather with family and friends to break the day's fast is an especially important event during Ramadan. Some efforts to green Ramadan have focused on the type of food that is eaten during the evening meal, emphasizing the need for it to be raised and processed in ways that causes no harm to farmers, laborers, and the Earth while also following Islamic dietary requirements. For example, Whole Earth Meats – which originally began as a ministry of the interfaith organization, Faith in Place – works to provide meat for Ramadan and the general public that: comes from local farms; supports sustainable/biodynamic farming methods; treats animals humanely; practices humane slaughtering according to *zabiha-halal* guidelines; maintains quality processing; encourages low-impact practices; and develops interest free reinvestment policies for small farmers.[8]

Take another example of how ritual practices are used to accentuate today's water problems.[9] In New Mexico's South Valley, Roman Catholic leaders partnered with Native American leaders and various other community and religious groups to protest the problem of water grabs by developers that was intensifying in the area. The South Valley is comprised of small farms, many of which have been in operation for hundreds of years. Since New Mexico receives less than ten inches of water a year, farmers for centuries have relied on a series of irrigation ditches through which water flows from the Rio Grande River. Current competition for water for urban development in and around Albuquerque has meant that water rights are being bought up and diverted from agricultural purposes for "trendy" suburban housing and shopping ventures. In response, farmer and former long-time Protestant pastor, John Shipley approached Sister Joan Brown of Franciscan Ecology Ministry to help form a community-based spiritual response to the problem. What ensued was a South Valley San Isidro (patron saint of farmers and laborers) celebration to highlight the issues of food and water and farmland and concerns about development in the area.

Holy Family Catholic Church served as the beginning place for the celebration as the church has a San Isidro statue to which worshippers pray for the blessing of seeds and the harvest and protection of children and workers. From the church, participants walked along the banks of a local irrigation ditch, led by a parishioner who carried the San Isidro statue. Community members from a variety of backgrounds participated in the walk from the church along the ditch, where the group eventually stopped and gathered along the water where the church's priest offered a prayer and blessing: "You have made water as one of your beautiful gifts to us. We ask you to bless this irrigation ditch and make it a source of life, a source of refreshment, a source of cleanliness, and joy to all." (Ostrow and Rockeller 2007) Following the prayer, participants scattered flower petals into the ditch, music was played, and the group continued the walk to a central area in the South Valley where other community members and groups converged. There they were joined by indigenous leaders and tribal members who offered prayers and blessings for the land and water in the Pueblo Tewa language. The ceremony closed with an interfaith prayer. "The practice of observing this ritually in an act of worship in essence is the way we prepare ourselves for the struggle we're going to have to fight," stated Shipley (Ostrow and Rockeller 2007). Later, the group formed a petition presented to city officials that advocated for the preservation of farmland and the conversation of water.

Faith traditions and communities are responding to the global water crisis in other ways too. These include, for instance, involvement with public policy advocacy efforts, infrastructure reforms to make facilities more water conserving, including by altering food choices, and water restorative farming methods. To close, I spotlight a final faith-based water initiative, one that is attempting to reverse pollution and contamination wrought by industrial agriculture by working to restore the health of a watershed.

Restoring Plaster Creek

Plaster Creek Stewards is a coalition of secular and faith-based groups that are working to restore the Plaster Creek watershed in the metro area of Grand Rapids, Michigan. The organization originally began as a service learning project of the Christian liberal arts college, Calvin College, though now it includes broad community partners, including Trout Unlimited, West Michigan Environmental Action Council (WMEAC), the Lower Grand River Organization of Watersheds (LGROW), the Christian Reformed Church in North America (whose headquarters are located near the banks of Plaster Creek), the Kent Conservation District, local schools and faith communities (referred to as "watershed schools" and "watershed faith communities"), and the local Islamic Center and Mosque. Covering 58 square miles, Plaster Creek is considered the most polluted stream in Western Michigan and among the most polluted in the state. By the year 2000, Plaster Creek held bacterial levels so high that it was considered unfit for even minimal human body contact (Heffner (with Warners and Ryskamp) 2013).

Called Kee-No-Shay, or "water of the walleye" by the region's Native American Odaawaa (Ottawa) inhabitants, Plaster Creek's history of degradation reaches back to the late nineteenth century. Legend has it that in the early 1800s Odaawaa leader, Chief Blackbird took a Baptist missionary in a small boat to float the creek, where they came upon a waterfall cascading over a beautiful, colorful stone, now known as gypsum that the missionary had never encountered. A sacred site for the Odaawaa, the missionary nevertheless took a sample of the gypsum and had it sent to a geologist in Detroit, who discovered that the rock could be ground into a base for plaster and fertilizer. The creek subsequently became a mine for gypsum, with the first plaster mill in Western Michigan built in 1841 near that same sacred site.

Known as Plaster Creek ever since, the stream originates in the agricultural area of Dutton and Caledonia and feeds into the Grand River, which eventually runs into Lake Michigan at the lakeshore town of Grand Haven. As records show, the watershed's hydrology was altered dramatically in the early 1900s when European settlers changed the landscape from native habitat to an active agricultural area (Plaster Creek Watershed Management Plan 2008, 16). Additionally, the ongoing urbanization of the watershed has made stormwater runoff – water that flows over land and concrete instead of being absorbed into soil – the creek's most significant causes of degradation. Plaster Creek Stewards have identified the following predominant pollutants and their sources. Note the agricultural source of many of them:

Sediment: Stormwater runoff causes flooding in Plaster Creek, which erodes stream banks and washes sediment into the creek. Sediment can also be introduced into the stream by runoff from agriculture and construction sites. Overabundant sediment in the creek blankets the creekbed and destroys habitat for fish and other aquatic life. It is also carried into the Grand River and Lake Michigan.

E. coli contamination: We know that *E. coli* contamination is a problem in Plaster Creek, but we don't know how exactly it gets there. Possible sources include dumping pet-waste down storm drains, leaky septic tanks, agricultural sources (livestock, manure), waste from wild animals, and many others. The sources of *E. coli* are not well understood, but it's clear that stormwater runoff from all parts of the watershed – both urban and rural and everything in between – is making the *E. coli* problem worse.

Nutrient pollution: Excess nutrients from lawn fertilizers, agricultural outputs, and animal manure can cause algae to bloom, compromising stream quality and degrading ecosystems downstream.

Thermal pollution: Runoff from warm, paved surfaces causes creek temperatures to fluctuate dramatically, making it inhospitable for native fish and other aquatic wildlife.

Toxic substances: The creek is contaminated by untreated urban runoff, road salt, and pesticides. Old industrial sites in the watershed may also be leaching legacy pollutants into the stream.[10]

Much of Plaster Creek Stewards' work focuses on community-based restoration efforts related to education about and installation of alternative stormwater solutions, including rain gardens, bio-swales, and buffers, all of which use the introduction of native landscaping as a way to absorb and divert water pollutants and sediment so they cannot reach the stream, especially during times of flooding. Farmers and landowners whose land abuts the creek are encouraged to plant trees, shrubs, grasses, and wildflowers along tributary and stream banks as a natural way to reduce soil erosion and sedimentation runoff, provide shade which cools the water, and filter harmful nutrients from livestock waste, pesticides, and fertilizers.

Plaster Creek Stewards operatives a native plant nursery, where they cultivate seedlings from hundreds of local varieties, many of which are rare or threatened. They also work to collect native seeds, which are then "overwintered" outdoors for three months and eventually brought into their greenhouses to germinate and plant. In the fall of 2016, they collected seeds from 470 native West Michigan species.[11] As a volunteer, community-based organization, the watershed restoration work that the Plaster Creek Stewards have accomplished is impressive. A fall 2016 event boasted the following:

100+ energetic volunteers including...
4 schools/church youth groups installed...
8 new curb-cut rain gardens planted with...
2,300 biodiverse, native plants (strong survivors) which began rooting in...
2 neighborhoods to infiltrate...
794,000 gallons of dirty runoff equivalent to...
(1.2 Olympic-sized swimming pools) each year from...
0.88 acres of urban landscape.[12]

Plaster Creek Stewards work to create the cultural change necessary for West Michigan residents to adopt a "downstream, upstream ethic" and instill a deep sense of care about their particular watershed and place is far from over. "It has taken Plaster Creek over 100 years to achieve the degraded condition it is in today and it will require several decades to restore it," they state, "but we are seeing growing interest among West Michigan residents to learn what they can do to care for their particular place. As momentum continues to build we are cultivating the hope that one day the walleye will return, and the creek's name can be changed back to Kee-No-Shay" (Heffner (with Warners and Ryskamp) 2013).

Even as watershed restoration efforts such as these represent "stopgap" measures in the sense that they do not work fundamentally to change the agricultural system that precipitated the water pollution in the first place, they will nevertheless become increasingly important as societies transition to developing more sustainable forms of agriculture in the face of global climate change. As I have written elsewhere, human society is presently entering a new era – namely, an era of restoration. Beyond entering an ecological age or a climate age in general, we are entering one particularly marked by the deliberate creative and systematic attempts of humans to restore the natural world and our connections to it. New forms of agriculture edged by restoration of the ecological degradation caused by agriculture's old ways will be the necessary tag team for the future health of our planet. Chapter 6 further accentuates this point.

Notes

1 See "Agriculture at a Crossroads," www.globalagriculture.org/report-topics/water.html (accessed May 1, 2017).
2 See the Water.org website, https://water.org/ (accessed June 8, 2017).
3 See The World Bank, http://www.worldbank.org/en/topic/water/projects (accessed May 19, 2017).
4 See GreenFaith Water Shield webpage, www.greenfaith.org/programs/greenfaith-shield/greenfaith-water-shield (accessed June 2, 2017).
5 See, for example, the citing of the problems in "Jewish Teachings on Water," GreenFaith: Water Shield. Available at http://www.faithinwater.org/uploads/4/4/3/0/44307383/jewish_teachings_on_water-greenfaith.pdf (accessed June 2, 2017).
6 See GreenFaith "Welcome to our Muslim GreenWorship Resource!" webpage, www.greenfaith.org/resource-center/spirit/greenworship-resource/muslim-greenworship-resource (accessed June 5, 2017).
7 The other pillars are declaration of faith, daily prayer, alms-giving, and pilgrimage to Mecca.
8 Whole Earth Meats website, www.wholeearthmeats.com/about-us/ (accessed June 9, 2017).
9 This example comes from the documentary film, *Renewal: Stories from America's Religious-Environmental Movement* (2007).
10 See Plaster Creek Stewards webpage, "What's wrong with Plaster Creek," www.calvin.edu/admin/provost/pcw/learn/status (accessed June 3, 2017).
11 See the Plaster Creek Stewards "Fall 2016 Newsletter," http://us10.campaign-archive2.com/?u=3398a5e58cc806aa226225a28&id=039f9186e5&e=%5BUNIQID (accessed May 23, 2017).
12 Ibid.

References

Ahmad, H. (2015a) *Islam and Water: The Hajjar (r.a.) Story and Guide*, Global One, London.
Ahmad, H. (2015b) *Islamic Farming: A Toolkit for Conservation*, Global One, London. Available at www.arcworld.org/downloads/Islamic-Farming-Toolkit.pdf (accessed June 1, 2017).
Baker, L. (2016) "In Colorado, farmers and cities battle over water rights," National Public Radio's All Things Considered, May 28, 2016. Available at www.npr.org/2016/05/28/479866079/colorado-towns-farmers-battle-over-water-rights (accessed May 19, 2017).
Barlow, M. (2013) *Blue Future: Protecting Water for People and the Planet Forever*, The New Press, New York, NY.
Brown, L. (1997) *The Agricultural Link: How Environmental Damage Could Disrupt Economic Progress*. Worldwatch Paper N. 136, Worldwatch Institute, Washington, DC.

Deutsch, L., Falkenmark, M., Gordon, L., Rochström, J., and Folke, C. (2010) "Water-mediated ecological consequences of intensification and expansion of livestock production," in H. Steinfeld, Mooney, H.A., Schneider, F., and Neville, L.E. (eds.), *Livestock in a Changing Landscape: Drivers, Consequences, and Responses*, Island Press, Washington, DC, 97–110.

Greenberg, P. (2013) "A river runs through it," *The American Prospect*, May 22, 2013. Available at http://prospect.org/article/river-runs-through-it (accessed June 12, 2017).

Harper, F. (n.d.) "Christian teaching on water," GreenFaith: Water Shield. Available at www.greenfaith.org/files/water-shield/christian-essay-and-discussion (accessed June 2, 2017).

Heffner, G.G. (with Warners, D. and Ryskamp, M) (2013) "Caring for a shared place: Restoring the water of the walley," *The Rapidian*, December 13, 2013. Available at http://www.therapidian.org/caring-shared-place-restoring-water-walley-now-known-plaster-creek (accessed May 23, 2017).

Michalak, A.M., et al. (2013) "Record-setting algal bloom in Lake Erie caused by agricultural and meteorological trends consistent with expected future conditions," *Proceedings of the National Academy of Sciences of the United States of America*, 110(16), 6448–6452. Available at www.pnas.org/content/110/16/6448.full?sid=51a83b45-31b0-4725-a477-84318d93a974 (accessed May 8, 2017).

Ostrow, M. and Rockeller, T.K. (Producers and Directors) (2007) *Renewal: Stories from America's Religious-Environmental Movement* [Documentary]. United States: Fine Cut Productions.

Peppard, C. Z. (2014) *Just Water: Theology, Ethics, and the Global Water Crisis*, Orbis Books, Maryknoll, NY.

Plaster Creek Watershed Management Plan. (2008) Available at www.calvin.edu/admin/provost/pcw/learn/Plaster%20Creek%20WMP.pdf (accessed October 26, 2017).

Schindler, D. and Vallentyne, J. (2008) *The Algal Bowl: Overfertilization of the World's Freshwaters and Estuaries*, rev. ed., EarthScan, New York, NY.

Troster, L. (n.d.) "Jewish teachings on water," GreenFaith: Water Shield. Available at www.faithinwater.org/uploads/4/4/3/0/44307383/jewish_teachings_on_water-greenfaith.pdf (accessed June 2, 2017).

United Nations Department of Economic and Social Affairs. (2015) Water for Life: 2005–2015. Available at www.un.org/waterforlifedecade/quality.shtml (accessed June 17, 2017).

Vallentyne, J. (1974) *The Algal Bowl: Lakes and Man*, Department of the Environment, Ottawa.

6

CLIMATE

Religion and food for a hot planet

Most often when we think about global climate change, energy and transportation first come to mind – coal burning power plants, solar wind farms, fossil fuels emitted by automobiles and jet planes, and fracking. But what about the connection between food and a warming planet, how do these fit together? Previous chapters have touched on some of the connections between current agricultural practices and climate change; this chapter examines them more explicitly. In doing so it considers how some religious groups have incorporated considerations of food and agriculture in developing faith-based responses to the current climate crisis. At the end, I spotlight two agricultural initiatives that interpret climate friendly farming methods as promising practices for reconnecting people, ecologically and culturally, to Earth.

How agriculture impacts climate

The International Panel on Climate Change (IPCC) breaks down emissions according to carbon dioxide equivalence as follows: 25.9 percent comes from energy supply, 19.4 percent from industry, 17.4 percent from forestry, 13.5 percent from agriculture, 13.1 percent from transport, 7.9 percent from residential and commercial buildings, and 2.8 percent from waste and wastewater. Yet as Anna Lappé points out in her 2010 book, *Diet for a Hot Planet: The Climate Crisis at the End of Your Fork and What You Can Do About It*, the IPCC figures hide agriculture's true climate footprint. For if we consider the *total* food process – from production to processing to distribution to consumption to waste – agriculture contributes to the greenhouse gas emissions of all of the above sectors. "Add all these slivers together," suggests Lappé, "and the entire global food chain may account for roughly one third of what's heating our planet" (Lappé 2010, 11).

Consider two examples cited by Lappé.[1] First is livestock production. Eighteen percent of total global greenhouse gas emissions, one tenth of carbon emissions, more than one third of methane emissions, and nearly two thirds of nitrous oxide emissions come from this agricultural practice alone. Even as carbon dioxide is responsible for the majority (76.7 percent) of global warming emissions, and methane and nitrous oxide for only 14.3 percent and 7.9 percent respectively, methane and nitrous oxide have a significantly higher global warming potential. Over the course of 100 years, methane is 23 times more potent and nitrous oxide 296 times more potent than carbon dioxide.

As we saw in Chapter 4, concentrated animal feeding operations (CAFOs) in particular are responsible for generating enormous amounts of global warming gases. The U.S. Environmental Protection Agency (EPA) defines CAFOs as facilities that confine animals for at least 45 days a year and do not produce their own feed. Classified as "farms" rather than "factories" CAFOs are not subject to the same environmental regulations as other climate polluting industries. This is significant for how climate polluting current large-scale animal agricultural practices are throughout the entire process, from the type and amount of feed required, to the animal waste produced, to the energy, land, and water used.

Recall the sheer volume of CAFOs. A large cattle CAFO may hold 1,000 or more animals, a hog CAFO may hold upwards of 2,500 swine, and a poultry operation may hold more than 125,000 birds. Livestock in CAFOs do not pasture or eat things they would normally eat, which means that they require an enormous amount of feed inputs, including corn, soybeans, and other foodstuffs, such as fishmeal. Ninety percent of all soy and half of all corn – one third of the world's cereal harvest – is used to feed animals on industrial farms. In the United States alone, two thirds of corn and 80 percent of soy goes not to feeding people, but to feeding animals. Of this, 19 percent is exported with much of this going to feed livestock in other parts of the world.

From producing feed for animal production to raising livestock, more than two thirds of the planet's arable land and a quarter of the total ice-free land surface is used for livestock. The upshot is that as the global demand for meat has steadily continued to rise over the past decade, agribusinesses are buying up large tracts of land all over the world, converting them from biodiverse forests and woodlands to agricultural lands for feed crop and livestock production. Such land grabbing for livestock production expansion has been particularly severe in Latin America where three quarters of the Amazon's forestland has been converted for livestock purposes. Nearly three quarters of Brazil's greenhouse gas emissions (Brazil is now among the world's leading meat exporters) stem from agribusiness expansion for livestock production.

On top of undermining biodiversity, a necessary ecological component for mitigating climate change, livestock grazing can lead to soil compaction and erosion, which releases carbon into the atmosphere that soils had previously been storing naturally. Further degrading biodiversity is the fact that livestock animals contribute to global species concentration, making up 88 percent of the volume of the world's total animal population, wild and domesticated. And seed concentration follows. The more animals raised for human consumption the greater need for monoculture feed crops such as corn and soy. Then there is the reliance on fossil fuels to produce synthetic fertilizers and power machinery used in livestock feed production. In the United States and Canada, half of synthetic fertilizer is used for feed crop production. For these reasons, Indian economist and chair of the IPCC, Rajendra Pachauri suggests that, "In terms of immediacy of action and the feasibility of bringing about reductions in a short period of time" choices regarding meat eating are "one of the most important personal choices we can make to address climate change" (as cited in Lappé 2010, xvii).

Yet as Lappé reveals, it is not only livestock production where food's deep climate impacts are evident. Consider palm oil. Contained in foods from granola bars to crackers to cream cheese to candy bars, as well as numerous health and cleaning products, the growth in the palm oil industry has been exponential over the past several decades, to the point that palm oil now leads the market in globally traded vegetable oils. Originally produced by small-scale farmers in western Africa, Dutch colonists and the British introduced palm oil to Java and Malaysia in the late nineteenth century. Today palm oil is mostly grown in Indonesia and Malaysia, where rainforests are being clear-cut and converted to massive palm plantations in order to keep up with global demand. In the process, biodiverse forest ecosystems are being destroyed at record pace undermining land's natural capacity to absorb carbon, as well as producing more of it. This becomes especially prevalent when considering the draining of the region's peat bogs for palm agricultural purposes.

Peatlands represent only 0.02 percent of ecosystems worldwide, though are incredibly efficient at storing and sequestering carbon. Containing trees that can reach 50 meters tall and hold millions of years of organic material, when peat bogs are drained and dried up for agricultural purposes, the oxidation process actually begins emitting rather than storing carbon. So powerful at absorbing carbon are peat bogs that if just one peatland area in Indonesia – the size of only 2 percent of the United States' total arable land – were completely destroyed, the carbon emitted would match that of the entire planet for a year. In rankings of the world's highest carbon emitting countries, Indonesia is often ranked in the twenties. But as Wetlands International points out, if the destruction of peat bogs were considered in the equation, Indonesia would rise in the rankings to number three (Lappé 2010, 30). And then there are the carbon-emitting fires, lasting at times for months that are more likely to occur when peatlands are drained and dried out.

As with the livestock and seed sectors, palm production is predominantly controlled by the world's largest agribusinesses, with small-scale palm farmers pushed out as corporations continue to buy up more and more land. Ten companies control two thirds of palm production in Indonesia, with Archer Daniels Midland and Cargill among the largest. Minnesota-based Cargill is the world's largest importer of palm oil in the United States. Add to both livestock and palm production the carbon-intensive cost of global trade and transportation. In 2007, the United States imported 10 million hogs and 2.5 million cattle from Mexico and Canada for domestic production on American feedlots. Poland today imports most of its livestock feed, including from places as far as Brazil. In 2008, the United States imported 2.5 billion pounds of veal and beef while at the same time exporting 1.9 billion pounds of the same meat, all of which requires energy intensive refrigeration for transportation. Moreover, palm oil containing products – most of which are packaged in plastic that requires additional energy to produce and eventually winds up in a landfill which produces even more warming gasses – can be purchased in virtually every grocery store and gas station, large and small, worldwide. From production to processing to distribution to consumption to waste, as these two examples show, our current food practices are contributing in far reaching ways to our planet's warming.

Burdens and benefits of agriculture's climate impacts

For most of us living in the Global North the climate consequences wrought by agriculture's current practices are minimal compared to those living in the Global South. We are, as we saw in the previous chapter, not "all in this together" in terms of how we directly experience the day to day realities of Earth's degradation. As with water, the global disparities and injustices associated with climate change are especially acute, particularly when we consider future projections about the regions and populations that will be most negatively impacted. *The 2007/8 Human Development Report: Fighting Climate Change: Human Solidarity in a Divided World* states that the consequences of climate change will be most deleterious for the world's poor and for future generations. Large parts of Africa, small island states, and coastal zones will see extreme weather, flooding, and drought in our lifetime, phenomena we have already begun to witness. For the world's poorest people, the report predicted, the effects of climate change could be "apocalyptic."[2]

So too climate change is expected to impact agricultural production variously around the world, with some regions faring much worse and others faring better. The IPCC predicts that with the planet warming just one to three degrees Celsius above 1990 levels, the agricultural capacity of low-latitude, equatorial, hot regions will be most negatively impacted.[3] Regions in Latin America and Africa that rely heavily on rainfall for agriculture will see significant reduction in crop yields. By 2020, some regions in Africa are expected to see crop reduction of up to 50 percent. Some high latitude temperate regions are, nonetheless, expected to see increases in crop yields with rising temperatures. In some rain fed agricultural areas in North America, for instance, crop yields are expected to increase 5 to 20 percent.

Still, data predicting climate impacts on agriculture in regions in the Global South is limited, as noted in a report of the International Centre for Trade and Sustainable Development (ICTSD), *Climate Change and Developing Country Agriculture*. Where region specific case studies do exist, they tend to focus on a limited number of cereal crops in a small area, making wider generalizability difficult. What is clear from the data is just how much harder hit the world's southern regions will be. The estimates include the following: Sub-Saharan Africa's rain-fed wheat, maize, rice production will decrease by 12 percent (net loss) by 2080, with great regional variations; Latin America's overall grain yields will change between -30 percent to +5 percent by 2080, with rain-fed wheat production decreasing by 12 to 27 percent by 2080; South Asia's net cereal production will decrease by at least 4 to 10 percent, with rain-fed wheat production decreasing by 20 to 75 percent by 2080; South East Asia's overall cereal production will increase by up to 30 percent, but rain-fed wheat production will decrease by 10 to 95 percent by 2080. Contrast consequences for the world's northern regions: Europe's cereal yields will increase in northern areas with rain-fed wheat production up by 10 to 30 percent, and will decrease in southern areas by 2080, however there will be a net gain overall; North America's yields will increase by 5 to 20 percent such as corn, rice, sorghum, soybean, wheat, common forages, cotton, and some fruits (Keane 2009, 2–3).

Not only is climate change projected to significantly undermine global food security for the world's poorest regions and people, so too, as we saw with the livestock and palm oil cases, it is seriously compromising the planet's biodiversity, ecosystem health, and species' diversity. In 2011, NASA published a map of the globe focusing on climate change's ecological impacts. By 2100:

> The model projections paint a portrait of increasing ecological change and stress in Earth's biosphere, with many plant and animal species facing increasing competition for survival, as well as significant species turnover, as some species invade areas occupied by other species. Most of Earth's land that is not covered by ice or desert is projected to undergo at least a 30 percent change in plant cover – changes that will require humans and animals to adapt and often relocate.
>
> In addition to altering plant communities, the study predicts climate change will disrupt the ecological balance between interdependent and often endangered plant and animal species, reduce biodiversity and adversely affect Earth's water, energy, carbon and other element cycles.
>
> *(Buis 2011)*

The article goes on to state that such shifting ecological dynamics may not always present negative consequences (take increased forestland in some parts of the Great Lakes region which means great carbon sequestration and wildlife habitat), which is also the case for agricultural production. What remains uncertain and unpredictable is how such shifts will impact historically evolved interdependent entities and systems and the Earth's balance on the whole.

Religious statements on climate change: agriculture's eclipse

Given the extent to which current agricultural and eating practices contribute to and are conversely impacted by Earth's warming it is remarkable to note, as does

Lappé, that of the 4,000 articles published in 16 top newspapers on climate change between 2005 and 2008, only 2.4 percent examined the impact of the food system, with just half of 1 percent focusing substantially on food and agriculture (as cited in Lappé 2010, xvi). The same could be said about religious responses to climate change. For even as numerous religious traditions, denominations, and groups have issued statements on the moral and spiritual significance of human induced global warming, few cite current agricultural and food practices as a root part of the problem. This could be because most religious climate statements tend to be brief and general and are intended to provide a kind of "blanket" statement that covers many issues. Still, it is difficult to find a religious response to global climate change that does not explicitly address the issues of energy and transportation, raising questions about agriculture's eclipse. There are nevertheless exceptions, and we note several of them here.

Laudato Si': On Care for Our Common Home

More than any other religious climate statement, Pope Francis' 2015 encyclical, *Laudato Si'* provides the most comprehensive treatment of the social and ecological problems associated with current agricultural practices. Its length at 82 pages could be part of the reason, yet I suspect that it has more to do with the fact that Francis' home place of Argentina has over the past two decades witnessed dramatic shifts in the agricultural landscape, including, most notably, the expansion of large-scale multinational corporate farming operations. Chapters 1 ("What Is Happening to Our Common Home") and 3 ("The Human Roots of the Ecological Crisis") of the encyclical deal most explicitly with agriculture's climate interface. Francis (2015) writes that the "vicious cycle" of global warming on the carbon cycle affects "the availability of essential resources like drinking water, energy and agricultural production in warmer regions, and leading to the extinction of part of the planet's biodiversity... Things are made worse by the loss of tropical forests which would otherwise help to mitigate climate change" (19–20). An entire section is dedicated to the issues of water, including how the increasing lack of fresh water impedes agricultural activity and industrial agricultural activities conversely pollute waterways. Later in the encyclical, when discussing the problem of human intervention in ecosystems, agriculture is cited as an example: "many birds and insects which disappear due to synthetic agrotoxins are helpful for agriculture: their disappearance will have to be compensated for by yet other techniques which may well prove harmful" (26).

Francis calls for greater analysis of "The replacement of virgin forest with plantations of trees, usually monocultures," which "can seriously compromise a biodiversity which the new species being introduced does not accommodate. Similarly, wetlands converted into cultivated land lose the enormous biodiversity which they formerly hosted" (29). Certain highly biodiverse areas need greater global protection, states *Laudato Si'* including the Amazon and the Congo basin, great aquifers and glaciers, for "when these forests are burned down or levelled for purposes of cultivation, within the space of a few years, countless species are lost and the areas frequently become arid wastelands" (28).The encyclical critiques overfishing which leads to "a drastic depletion of certain species" and the destruction of coral reefs at the hand of pollution from deforestation and agricultural monocultures is also noted (29, 30).

Laudato Si' does not cite outright a moral problem with GMOs, though it does raise concerns about how the expansion of GM crops by "oligopolies" negatively impacts small farmers and destroys complex ecosystem networks and seed biodiversity (99–100). It calls out multinational corporations for doing things in the developing world that "they would never do in developed countries or the so-called first world," including contributing to local agricultural decline. Francis critiques what he calls the "globalization of the technocratic paradigm," noting that collectives of small producers may provide an alternative paradigm that emphasizes community and a non-consumeristic way of life. Small-scale agriculture is also mentioned in relation to the need to promote a diverse economy and business creativity. Francis calls on civic leaders to support the expansion of small-scale, diversified food production systems (95–96).

The alternative paradigm proposed in *Laudato Si'* is one of "integral ecology" which respects the interrelated character of Earth, including the human and social dimension. Here Francis notes the importance of privileging the "cultural ecology" of indigenous peoples who he views as "not merely one minority among others" but "principal dialogue partners, especially when large projects affecting their land are proposed" (110). Francis strongly critiques the "huge consumption" of some in rich countries for how it negatively impacts the world's poorest areas, particularly in Africa where droughts are devastating farmers.

Action items in the document are weak on agriculture, though do suggest the need for international dialogue that could lead to planning for a sustainable and diversified agriculture (122). Francis emphasizes the need for dialogue for new national and local policies and transparency in decision making, suggesting that political activity on the local level could be directed at

> protecting certain species and planning a diversified agriculture and the rotation of crops. Agriculture in poorer regions can be improved through investment in rural infrastructures, a better organization of local or national markets, systems of irrigation, and the development of techniques of sustainable agriculture. New forms of cooperation and community organization can be encouraged in order to defend the interests of small producers and preserve local ecosystems from destruction. Truly, much can be done!
>
> *(132–33)*

The final chapter on ecological and spirituality is surprisingly weak on agriculture and food. It advocates for a "new lifestyle" marked by simplicity and sobriety, which focuses on reduction of consumeristic behaviors, rather than on making climate friendly food choices. One section suggests, "avoiding the use of plastic and paper, reducing water consumption, separating refuse, cooking only what can reasonably be consumed, showing care for other living beings, using public transport or car-pooling, planting trees, turning off unnecessary lights, or any number of other practices" (155). Still, even in the document's final section on the sacraments of the Eucharist and Sabbath rest – both practices which are ripe for agricultural interpretation as they center on food and the breaking bread in community – food is only mentioned in a mystical, cosmic sense. Nevertheless, *Laudato Si'* provides the most significant current example of a religious document on climate change that specifically addresses the consequences of industrial agriculture on warming planetary conditions. Moreover, it emphasizes the environmental ethical and social justice issues pointed up by today's agricultural system, even as it surprisingly neglects food and farming's spiritual dimensions.

Statement of the Evangelical Climate Initiative

As with *Laudato Si'*, the Statement of the Evangelical Climate Initiative states that global climate change is among the most critical moral issues faced by people of faith today. Issued in 2006, the document has been endorsed by 86 leading Christian evangelical pastors, scholars, and organizations, including Rick Warren, author of *The Purpose Driven Life*, Calvin DeWitt, professor of Environmental Studies at the University of Wisconsin-Madison, and Richard Cizik, president of the New Evangelical Partnership for the Common Good. Much shorter than *Laudato Si'* at just three pages, the document is worth noting for how it addresses agriculture as a root cause of climate change, and for how it provides an example of environmental engagement by evangelical Christians, a group that has generally been more skeptical of anthropogenic climate change than other Christians as well as the general public. Similar to *Laudato Si'* the document stresses the disproportionate negative impacts climate change will have on the world's poorest communities and regions, including in terms of agricultural production. It states:

> Even small rises in global temperatures will have such likely impacts as: sea level rise; more frequent heat waves, droughts, and extreme weather events such as torrential rains and floods; increased tropical diseases in now-temperate regions; and hurricanes that are more intense. It could lead to significant reduction in agricultural output, especially in poor countries. Low-lying regions, indeed entire islands, could find themselves under water. (This is not to mention the various negative impacts climate change could have on God's other creatures.)
>
> *(2006)*

A section on Christian moral responsibility to respond to the problem of climate change does not explicitly address food and agriculture, though it could be inferred in several of the document's theological principles. These include the beliefs that the world belongs to God and that any damage done to God's Earth is done to God's very self; Christians are called to love their neighbors as themselves and "to

protect and care for the least of these as though each was Jesus Christ himself";
and "Christians, noting the fact that most of the climate change problem is human
induced, are reminded that when God made humanity he commissioned us to
exercise stewardship over the earth and its creatures" (2006).

The document's final "claim" (this is the term used for each of the four sections)
states that "the need to act now is urgent" (2006). It calls on governments, busi-
nesses, churches, and individuals to take action. In a rather odd twist compared to
the rest of the document's tenor and focus, the statement recommends "cap-and-
trade" policy as preferable in terms of promoting carbon emissions reduction. It
commends, by name, particular senators and corporations that have taken positive
steps to combat climate change, including "BP, Shell, General Electric, Cinergy,
Duke Energy, and DuPont, all of which have moved ahead of the pace of government action through innovative measures implemented within their companies in
the U.S. and around the world" (2006).

Unlike *Laudato Si'* the evangelical statement makes no mention of creation-
oriented spirituality or the joy of simple living, food oriented or otherwise. It
is interesting to note, however, that the Christians and Climate site where the
Evangelical statement is housed includes an additional article advocating the adoption of climate friendly food.[4] The article specifically notes the connection between
food choices and climate change, stating, "It's no longer about the type of cars people are driving or their energy conservation efforts. Focus is now shifting towards
the foods you consume." It critiques factory farming for its reliance on fossil fuels,
and instead suggests a vegetable rich diet.

Islamic Declaration on Global Climate Change

The Islamic Declaration on Global Climate Change was launched on August 18, 2015
at the International Islamic Climate Change Symposium held in Istanbul, Turkey as
part of a collaborative effort of Islamic Relief Worldwide, Islamic Foundation for
Ecology and Environmental Sciences (IFEES), and GreenFaith. Endorsed by Muslim
leaders from 20 countries, including the grand muftis of Lebanon and Uganda, the
declaration was intentionally issued just prior to the 2015 Paris Climate Change
Conference. The document opens with the following preamble:

> Excessive pollution from fossil fuels threatens to destroy the gifts bestowed
> on us by God gifts such as a functioning climate, healthy air to breathe, regu-
> lar seasons, and living oceans. But our attitude to these gifts has been short
> sighted, and we have abused them. What will future generations say of us,
> who leave them a degraded planet as our legacy? How will we face our Lord
> and Creator?
>
> *(2015)*

It continues by citing Millennium Ecosystem Assessment (UNEP, 2005) and IPCC
(March 2014) concerns, concluding with *Laudato Si'* and the evangelical statement

that the brunt of climate change devastation will fall on the poor. Different from these documents, the Islamic Declaration notes how climate change will negatively impact "countless other creatures." Similarly, agricultural reference can be read into the declaration's theological affirmations, which stress the built-in balance, fertility, and seasonal cycles of God's created order:

> God created the earth in equilibrium (mīzān); By His immense mercy we have been given fertile land, fresh air, clean water and all the good things on Earth that make our lives here viable and delightful; The earth functions in natural seasonal rhythms and cycles: a climate in which living beings – including humans – thrive; The present climate change catastrophe is a result of the human disruption of this balance.
>
> *(2015, 4)*

Climate change is a consequence of corruption (fasād) in the "relentless pursuit of economic growth and consumption," states the declaration. Additional consequences include land and water pollution, soil erosion, deforestation and desertification, the destruction and degradation of ecosystems, including Earth's most biodiverse systems such as coral reefs, wetlands, and rainforests, the introduction of genetically modified organisms, and damage to human health. More than *Laudato Si'* and the evangelical statement, the Islamic Declaration emphasizes the interrelated character of creation and how human beings are but one organism among many others, a realization that should motivate a sense of care for Earth and its beings: "We are but one of the multitude of living beings with whom we share the earth; We have no right to abuse the creation or impair it; Intelligence and conscience should lead us, as our faith commands, to treat all things with care and awe (taqwā) of their Creator, compassion (rahmah) and utmost good (ihsān)" (5). Moral responsibility for the care and protection of all living beings, the declaration states, is also affirmed in the teachings of Muhammad, who, states the declaration, "Ate simple, healthy food, which only occasionally included meat; Took delight in the created world; and Was, in the words of the Qur'an, "a mercy to all beings" (6).

Agriculture is not explicitly mentioned in the declaration's call to action, though can be inferred at several points. It incites well-off nations and oil-producing states to reduce consumption and unethical profit from the environment and preserve Earth's remaining resources for the elevation of the livelihood of the world's poorest people (6). It also calls on corporations, finance, and the business sector to change from the current growth oriented economy to a circular one that is entirely sustainable (7). The declaration concludes with the words of Muhammad: "We bear in mind the words of our Prophet (blessings and peace be upon him): The world is sweet and verdant, and verily Allah has made you stewards in it, and He sees how you acquit yourselves. (Hadīth related by Muslim from Abū Sa'īd Al-Khudrī)" (8).

Even as these three documents present positive examples of how religious views of climate change may include the consideration of agricultural and food issues, they also raise additional questions. For example: Why is the issue of meat eating neglected (save in the evangelical site's sidebar article), despite its huge impact on global climate change as we have seen? Why isn't the spirituality of eating practices highlighted, even as the sharing of food in community is a centerpiece in each of these faith traditions, and arguably a dimension that the religions have most to offer on the topic? And how, if at all, are documents such as these actually influencing the attitudes and behaviors of people of faith to make climate food friendly choices? These are just a few of the questions that will need to be addressed in future explorations of how faith traditions and communities are engaging the problem of climate change. For now, to conclude, we highlight two farming initiatives that are taking seriously the problem of climate and what needs to be done agriculturally to mitigate it.

Natural Systems Agriculture

Termed Natural Systems Agriculture (NSA) in 1977 by geneticist Wes Jackson and The Land Institute in Salina, Kansas which he founded, Jackson's premise is simple. For the past 10,000 years, agriculture has developed in ways that fundamentally degrade the soil, from the ancient Greeks to the civilizations of Mesopotamia to the Romans to the Americas (2002), with the last half century witnessing the most intensive soil degradation to date. Jackson cites studies by Cornell University scientist, David Pimentel's team: "In the four years prior to 1995 'nearly one-third of the world's arable land [has] been lost by erosion at a rate of more than 10 million hectares per year" (Jackson 2010, 8). As Jackson points out, "That is twenty-four million acres, half the size of Kansas" (8). New agricultural technologies such as no-till have reduced erosion, but still, as Jackson points out, even these methods are based on a systems of monoculture annual crops that require yearly planting and intensive amounts of nitrogen inputs in order to keep the soil and plants in place. Alternatively, Jackson proposes that societies reenvision agriculture based on the cultivation of perennials, varieties of plants that do not require replanting year to year.

Perennials have roots much deeper than annuals, and thus, are hardier and can filter and draw water from greater depths. Rather than degrade soils, perennial plants actually improve soil structure and protect it from erosion, increasing nutrient retention in ecosystems. Since perennials do not require replanting year to year, they too reduce other inputs (people and/or animal power, fuel, etc.) that are conventionally required to raise crops, additionally reducing adverse climate impacts. A sustainable agriculture, believes Jackson, will need to follow the patterns of evolutionary ecological systems themselves if humans hope to adapt to the particular ecosphere in which they find themselves. Ecological systems from tundra to desert to prairie to forest are predominantly comprised of perennials; so too should our agricultural systems.

And today, as Jackson's Land Institute has proven, we have reached the point scientifically that we can do it. Over the course of 40 years of research, the Institute has developed what they call "new hardware for agriculture" based on perennial seed crops and ecologically intensified polycultures that mimic natural systems. Humans have been domesticating wild perennials since the advent of agriculture (e.g., olive trees, grapes, asparagus, fruit trees). The Land Institute's work too is working to domesticate wild varieties, though instead it focuses on breeding wild perennial grains, legumes, and oilseed crops since these are the types of plants that currently dominate conventional agriculture and have the capacity to feed a growing global population. Among the most successful wild grains they have thus far bred is Kernza (*Thinopyrum intermedium*), which originates from a forage grass that is a cousin of wheatgrass. Different from annual wheat, Kernza's roots reach twice as far underground, some ten feet, and its seed head contains twice as many seeds. Kernza's seeds are currently one-fifth the size of an annual wheat seed, yet the Institute is working to increase the seed size to 50 percent the size of a wheat seed. Kernza is The Land Institute's first trademarked perennial grain to reach the commercial market (in 2017, the outdoor company Patagonia came out with a Kernza-based beer called "Deep Roots"), with others such as wild sorghum, wild wheat, wild rice, and wild sunflower in the process.

Jackson and The Land Institute firmly believe that perennial-based agriculture can be scaled globally to meet the needs of a growing human population on a warming planet. Their vision: "In the next forty years, we intend to develop an agricultural system featuring perennials with the ecological stability of the prairie and a grain and seed yield comparable to that from annual crops. Through such a system, we can produce ample human food and reduce or eliminate impacts from the disruptions and dependencies of industrial agriculture."[5]

Farming God's Way

Next consider an approach to climate friendly farming developed in sub-Saharan Africa with faith groups working on land and water conservation issues. Spearheaded by The Alliance of Religions and Conservation (ARC) founded in by Prince Phillip, the ARC began working in 2010 with Christian, Muslim, and Hindu groups in 11 African countries, launching a long-term environmental action plan in 2012 in Nairobi, Kenya. Farming God's Way grew out of this initiative and has since been enacted by Christian and Muslim groups across sub-Saharan Africa. The method combines climate smart conservation-based approaches to agriculture that are widely promoted throughout Africa with religious teachings about care for the Earth.

The Muslim Farming God's Way program, titled *Islamic Farming*, is spelled out in a training manual organized according to six "Ps" based on "the Promises of Allah: planning, prepare, plant, provide, protect, and produce (2005, 6). Rooted in historical farming methods that were developed during the Islamic agricultural revolution from the eighth century on in the Middle East and North Africa, the manual draws on the Arabic literary genre, the Books of Filāha, a compilation of hundreds of volumes on agriculture that have only recently been discovered in various places throughout the Muslim world, including Iraq, Egypt, Yemen, and Persia. The Books describe a scientific approach to agriculture and cover the topics of botany, agronomy, horticulture, and animal husbandry. Echoing what today is referred to as alternative, biodynamic, organic, sustainable, or regenerative farming,

Muslim agronomists during this time period stressed the importance of balancing the elements of soil, water, air, and manure/composting.

Four concerns characterized early Islamic agriculture: rules on land ownership and labor rights, irrigation methods, improved farming techniques, and the introduction of new crops. Many of these concerns, states the manual, translate to today's agricultural context in sub-Saharan Africa. Islamic rules on land ownership and labor rights, for example, speak to the recent problem of land grabbing by other countries and corporations, and instead suggest an equitable approach to land ownership where men and women (today 70 percent of farmers in Africa are women) can own and farm their own land. The spread of Islam throughout the Middle East and North Africa meant that Muslim communities inherited ancient irrigation systems that they then worked to repair and expand with methods such as the qanāt, a well-like water-management system that does not require a pump but uses gravity to transport large amounts of water across hot, arid landscapes, a system that could become increasingly valuable given global water shortages. Water use too was strictly regulated during the Islamic agricultural revolution, a practice that today could help mitigate the waste and misuse of water. Early Muslim farming almanacs detailed specific crops to grow in particular conditions, as well as how to grow healthy, fertile soil by adding organic matter such as manure and compost and rotating crops. Recent severe drought and water shortages across Africa, especially in the Horn of Africa, make such practices especially important. The cultural exchange that took place during Islamic unification included the introduction of new crops and plants, such as rice, saffron, and artichokes, and information about how to grow them. It also contributed to the development of a more diversified diet in the Muslim world that insured greater food security and health during times of distress, a concern particularly relevant in today's context.

Islamic Farming is guided by the following scriptural principles: *taqwa* (God consciousness), *tawakkul* (reliance on Allah), *salah* (prayers), *tawba* (repentance), and *infaq fisabillah* (charity). *Taqwa* refers to mindfulness and piety to live an ethical Muslim life, safeguarding one against sin. *Inshallah*, or "if God wills" connotes the idea of *tawakkul*, which emphasizes the Muslim belief in God as the sole creator and sustainer of the universe. *Tawba* is the spiritual practice of asking God for forgiveness and includes the belief that God continually forgives sins. Charity refers to the belief that the more a Muslim gives to those in need, the more blessings are returned to him/her from God.

Islamic Farming emphasizes "climate smart" organic farming, with an emphasis on creating a farm as an integrated, self-contained unit. It stresses the need to "know your soil" before planting and gives hands-on tips for testing the soil's chemical pH by, say, mixing in vinegar to see if it bubbles (if it does the soil is alkaline). Keeping livestock is recommended as a way to fertilize and recycle nutrients on fields and provide milk and meat for a family's diet, and animals should always be well cared for. No-till methods are preferred and the manual gives instructions for how to dig planting holes and build a composting operation. Mechanical tillage is not endorsed in *Islamic Farming* as it disturbs the soil and is less efficient than no-till (the manual points out that the Food and Agriculture Organization of the United Nations (FAO) suggests that no-till can save farmers 30–40 percent of their time). There should be a high quality of work when it comes to preparing and planting one's farm, the manual instructs: "An important message of Islamic Farming is that our farms should reflect our taqwa and the order and glory of Allah's creation...When we prepare our holes, they should be in beautiful straight lines. They should all be the same depth and width, and have the appearance of neatness and order" (40).

One-third of the farm should be legumes, which are excellent nitrogen-fixers and increase soil fertility; roots, shoots, and fruits should be rotated. Pests should be managed naturally by building the healthiest possible soil and, in extreme outbreaks, with home-made insecticides, such as teas made out of strong smelling plants (African marigold, garlic, onion, and chillies). Chemical fertilizers and/or pesticides should never be used. Instead, states the manual, thick mulch should be applied and weeds removed; companion planting and livestock can help. Burning is not an option in *Islamic Farming* as it is a short-term solution and will not ultimately build the health of soil. Collect seeds by letting the healthiest plants flower and dry out and then harvesting the seeds; it will save a lot of money. The manual concludes with a spiritual message about waste:

> Allah has given us abundant resources and we should not be wasteful. This is why we do not burn crop residues – it would be wasting. Similarly, we do not want to waste water and that is why we should apply thick mulch and capture rainwater from our roofs. We also do not want to waste the time that Allah has given to us. We should take action and not be lazy. We should be on time with our planning and with our preparing of holes, with planting, providing and protecting. Time is a precious resource that we should not waste.
>
> *(53)*

To conclude: Farming God's Way provides an interesting and instructive example of how religious groups are partnering with agricultural practitioners to develop programs that meet both practical and spiritual needs in efforts to adapt to climate change. It is significant for its emphasis on farmer and religious education, and for its itinerant character. Reminiscent of George Washington Carver's Jessup Wagon – which Carver called a "moveable school" for how it traveled from community to community to educate on agricultural matters – Farming God's Way provides a model that is replicable among climate conscious faith groups in various locales. In the following, final chapter, we examine three farms that are doing a kind of farming God's way that accentuate the symbolic, ritual significance of the growing and eating of food.

Notes

1 I am indebted to Lappé (2010, 3–41) for the analysis that follows in this section.
2 As cited on the Food, Energy, and Water: Environmental Issues from a Global Justice Perspective (FEW) website, http://www.fewresources.org/climate-roulette-were-not-all-in-this-together.html (accessed July 25, 2017).

3 Ibid.
4 See "Environmentally Friendly Food," June 4, 2016. Available at http://www.christian-sandclimate.org/environmentally-friendly-food/ (accessed October 5, 2017).
5 See the Land Institute website, https://landinstitute.org/about-us/vision-mission/ (accessed May 25, 2017).

References

Ahmad, H. (2015b) *Islamic Farming: A Toolkit for Conservation*, Global One, London. Available at http://www.arcworld.org/downloads/Islamic-Farming-Toolkit.pdf (accessed June 1, 2017).

Buis, A. (2011) "Climate change may bring big ecosystem changes," NASA: Global Climate Change: Vital Signs of the Planet, News, December 13, 2011. Available at https://climate.nasa.gov/news/645/climate-change-may-bring-big-ecosystem-changes/ (accessed July 28, 2017).

Francis, Pope. (2015) *Laudato Si: On Care for Our Common Home*, Vatican Press, Rome.

Islamic Declaration on Global Climate Change (2015) Available at http://www.ifees.org.uk/wp-content/uploads/2016/10/climate_declarationmMWB.pdf (accessed July 30, 2017).

Jackson, W. (2002) "Natural Systems Agriculture: A radical alternative," *Agriculture, Ecosystems and Environment*, Volume 88, 111–117.

Jackson, W. (2010) *Consulting the Genius of the Place: An Ecological Approach to a New Agriculture*, Counterpoint Press, Berkeley, CA.

Keane, J., Page, S., Kergna, A., and Kennan, J. (2009) *Climate Change and Developing Country Agriculture: An Overview of Expected Impacts, Adaptation and Mitigation Challenges, and Funding Requirements*, Issue Brief No. 2, December 2009, International Centre for Trade and Sustainable Development and International Food and Agricultural Trade Policy Council. Available at http://www.agritrade.org/Publications/documents/JKEANEweb_FINAL.pdf (accessed July 25, 2017).

Lappé, A. (2010) *Diet for a Hot Planet: The Climate Crisis at the End of Your Fork and What You Can Do About It*, Bloomsbury USA, New York, NY.

Millennium Ecosystem Assessment (UNEP) (2005) Ecosystems and human well-being: synthesis (PDF). Washington, DC: Island Press. (accessed September 15, 2017).

Statement of the Evangelical Climate Initiative (2006). Available at http://www.christiansandclimate.org/statement/ (accessed July 29, 2017).

7

THE NEW SACRED FARM

It is a warm September day and I am attempting to locate Mother Carr's Organic Farm in Lynwood, Illinois, where I am scheduled to meet with the farm's manager for a tour. West and south of Gary, Indiana by approximately 15 miles, Mother Carr's is an outreach ministry of Vernon Park Church of God, a 1,200-member African–American congregation that was founded in the mid-1950s on Chicago's south side. The farm is named after a particularly savvy and committed parishioner from that era, Mother Julia Carr, who planted a small Second World War victory garden to supplement food supplies during the war, and later started an inner-city garden for the community. The current farm was started several years ago by church member and now full-time farm manager Anthony Williamson, who had a vision for reviving Mother Carr's community gardening legacy when the congregation purchased 70 acres of former agricultural land to construct its new building, and eventually, a multiuse, intergenerational community, Vernon Park Village. Mother Carr's farm sits on approximately two of those 70 acres, a football field length behind the new church building. It boasts as one of the only African–American church-owned community-supported agriculture's (CSA's), and probably the only one with a bee operation for pollination and honey production.[1]

I exit highway 394 and take a right at the first main traffic light, then a left at the next major intersection, as Anthony had instructed me on the phone. On the south side of the road sits a cluster of greenhouses that I mistake for the church garden. Ahead there are more greenhouses, closed for the season, and then a large billboard, advertising the new site of Vernon Church of God with a photo of and message from the church's pastor. Just past the billboard, 200 yards off the road, I recognize the concrete silhouette of the new church based on a YouTube video on the church website I had watched the night before. Several large dump trucks shuttle back and forth down a dirt road that leads back behind the church.

I drive past the church still looking for the farm. Based on other community gardens I have visited, I am expecting to find some type of sign, however small and rough-hewn; but I find nothing. I call Anthony. He is on a farm errand and tells me to drive back to the area where the trucks are hauling dirt. To get there, he says, I need to find the opening in the chain-link fence, where a dirt construction road will lead me back to the farm behind the church building site. Once I get to the farm I will find a guy named Mark, he tells me. Anthony says he will call him to let him know that I am on my way.

I make a U-turn, pass the entrance once, turn around again, and finally find the opening in the fence that leads to the construction road. So much dust is flying up from the three dump trucks moving dirt that I can barely see ahead of my car. The road is rough, and I wonder whether the university loaned sedan I am driving is going to make it. I drive back to the church construction site where there sits a silver Vibe next to a porta john. There are two people sitting in the Vibe, and I stop and ask if they know where the farm is. "Nope," they say, "no idea." I drive farther back, still seeing nothing, despite the fact that it is a wide-open farm field. I continue to follow the dirt road, winding past the moving dump trucks and through the massive potholes. Nothing. I turn back toward the Vibe, which now I realize, is associated with the dump truck operation. The trucks have stopped, so I get out and ask the drivers whether they know of a farm. They say no, but they thought they saw someone way back past where they were working. So I get back in, and continue through the muck and potholes.

And sure enough, I find it. I also find Mark, a college student and farm intern, who is this afternoon picking green bush beans, which he is emptying into a large black garbage bag to take the next day to the church's CSA distribution day. I introduce myself and tell him that I am happy to help pick. He finds me a bucket and shows me where to go in the rows. We pick while he tells me about the farm.

Other than the rows of plants, which at this point of the season are filled with weeds, there is no fence, no markers, no trellises or chicken wire, just the garden growing in the middle of 70 acres of former industrial farmland. To the east sits a sizeable conventional garden nursery, vegetable farm, and cider mill, to the west, vacant farmland, and to the south, more vacant farmland and an industrial lot. The hum of car traffic on IL-394 can be seen and heard in the distance.

Most environmentalists, and religionists for that matter, would likely not accord sacred status to the type of isolated, semi-urban farm plot just described. Yet as we have seen through this book many in the food and faith movement do use language of the sacred, albeit in varied and diverse ways, to describe the types of practices and beliefs that orient their work. These include ritual, symbolic interpretations of agricultural and food practices, as well as accounts of the types of spiritual experiences they may yield. This final chapter explores some of these motifs by examining the work of three religious, community-based farms: Coastal Roots Farm in Encinitas, California, The Abundant Table in Ventura, California, and Mother Carr's Organic Farm in Lynwood, Illinois.[2]

Coastal Roots Farm is a Jewish farm associated with the progressive Jewish environmental organization, Hazon, as well as the San Diego north county Jewish Hub.[3] The farm's staff and volunteer base largely reflects Hazon's progressive Jewish theological orientation, though Coastal Roots also works with non-Jewish schools and organizations and attracts non-Jewish residents to farm festivals and events, broadening its demographic. Abundant Table is affiliated with the Episcopal Church and the Evangelical Lutheran Church of America (ELCA), as well as the Episcopal Service Corps Internship program. Like Coastal Roots Farm it involves school and volunteer groups and participants in its programs from the broader community.[4] Mother Carr's Organic Farm is a ministry of Mt. Vernon Church of God, an African–American congregation of the Protestant denomination, The Church of God. Its staff and volunteers are members of the congregation, though, as with the other two farms, Mother Carrs' is significantly involved with food activities in the wider Chicago area.[5]

Despite theological and demographic differences, each of these farms utilizes spiritual and ecological language to frame and describe their work. Oftentimes the interpretations enacted by these communities are shaped by beliefs and practices particular to the farm's particular faith tradition. Other times they are influenced by what I would consider more secular forms of environmental oriented spirituality.[6] It is the unique blending of narratives and meanings regarding the sacred quality of agricultural and food work that marks in my mind one of the more unique aspects of these farms – for now the sacred is neither confined to a particular religious tradition nor excluded from the broader public, rather, it is out in the open and hybridized, relocated, and reinterpreted in relation to the universal human experience of the need to grow food to eat.[7] Religious farms, I want to argue in this closing chapter, are producing new forms of ecological spirituality based on the experience of working with soil, plants, water, and collectively what Aldo Leopold called "the land." Below we explore some of the ritual practices central to these forms of land-based spirituality. But first a definitional step is in order, for in order to examine religious farm sites in sacred terms, we will need to know more about what is meant by the term "sacred" and how, in particular, it is used in understanding certain spaces.

Contested sacred space

Views of sacred space in the study of the history of religions have been interpreted in two primary ways.[8] On the one hand, thinkers such as Mircea Eliade have viewed particular places as sacred for how they manifest experiences of the really real (substantial view). On the other hand, theorists such as Johnathan Z. Smith argue that sacred spaces are products of historically and culturally specific ritual practices (contextual view). Referring to these two approaches as the poetics and the politics of sacred space respectively, religion scholars, David Chidester and Edward T. Linenthal, suggest that theorists have mostly engaged in the former type of analysis of sacred space, despite the fact that it is more accurate, in their minds, to analyze sacred spaces as places of struggle over the legitimate ownership of religious symbols, or, in other words, in political terms.[9]

Sacred spaces in America tend to exhibit several characteristics, according to Chidester and Linenthal. First, they involve rituals where "formalized repeatable symbolic performances" are enacted in ways that introduce extraordinary actions in otherwise ordinary environments (Chidester and Linenthal 1995, 9). These include embodied material practices, which oftentimes demarcate the way things "ought to be" in tension with the way they "actually are." Second, they are sites of reinterpretation that focus central questions about "what it means to be a human being in a meaningful world" (12). Reinterpretation also oftentimes involves the symbolic ordering and sacred significance of the natural and built environments, as well as the beings (human, superhuman, nonhuman) that inhabit them. Lastly, sacred spaces are inevitably contested sites defined by "negotiated contests over the legitimate ownership of sacred symbols" (15). This element focuses attention not only on how space has been "ritualized and interpreted but also to how it has been appropriated, contested, and 'stolen' back and forth in struggles over power in America."[10]

A final point from Chidester and Linenthal's (1995) analysis of sacred space is worth noting for our purposes. This is that the production of sacred space is generated in and through certain symbolic strategies, including the strategies of appropriation, exclusion, inversion, and hybridization. Most relevant to our task are the maneuvers of inversion and hybridization, for these best "lend themselves to projects of reversal, or innovation, or even to the kinds of 'desecration' that symbolize alternative relationships to sacred space" (19). Here "the high becomes low, the inside becomes outside, the peripheral becomes central" (19). Hybridization seems particularly apt: "found in practices of mixing, fusing, or transgressing conventional spatial relations…Such reversals and mixtures of dominant spatial relations produce new places, or reclaim old places, as a type of space that Foucault called a heterotopia, 'a kind of effectively acted utopia in which the real sites, all the 'other real sites that can be found within the culture, are simultaneously represented, contested, and inverted'" (19–20). Religious farm sites in America are ripe for the type of analysis of the production of sacred space that Chidester and Linenthal suggest. Taking their lead in terms of the characteristics that define sacred spaces in America, we begin by exploring some of the ritual practices enacted on religious farms sites.

Ritualization on the farm

Ritual studies scholar Catherine Bell proposes the term "ritualization" as "a way of acting that is designed and orchestrated to privilege what is being done in comparison to other, more quotidian activities…[It is] a matter of variously culturally specific strategies for setting some activities off from others, for creating and privileging a qualitative distinction between the 'sacred' and the 'profane'" (Bell 1992, 32–35).[11] In the case of faith-based farms, it is the mode of setting off and privileging the acts of farming and food work as qualitatively meaningful activities in themselves, in contrast to say, sitting and playing video games on a Saturday afternoon or going shopping at the mall. While one can scarcely get more mundane than turning dirt, spreading compost, sorting seeds, picking weeds, and harvesting and washing vegetables these activities are raised to the level of the meaningful work of agriculture when they are ritualized.[12]

Religious-oriented farm sites engage in the ritualization of agricultural and food practices in a variety of ways. Take the autumn, community-wide food festival organized at Coastal Roots Farm. "Sukkot on the Ranch," as it is called, celebrates the Jewish harvest festival, Sukkot, which also commemorates the 40-year period when the Israelites wandered in the desert, living in temporary built structures or "booths," the Hebrew meaning of the festival's name. A daylong event, Sukkot on the Ranch includes a wide range of intergenerational activities from puppet shows to DIY fermentation and Jewish food justice workshops.

Most of the day's activities at Sukkot on the Ranch involve hands-on experiential activities that put children and adults in direct, physical contact with soil and with one another. One workshop on fermentation led by a "Pickling Rabbi," instructed participants in the process of making from scratch sauerkraut and pickles from the farm's cabbage and cucumbers. A Jerusalem market, Machane Yehuda was recreated so that children could feel the atmosphere, pace, and energy of an Israeli market while learning about the *etrog, lulav,* and the four species of Sukkot. There were seed balls to mix and new recipes to learn. In a session titled "No SNAP Judgment," Jewish Family Service San Diego Hand Up Teen Leadership program led a cooking workshop using recipes from the SNAP cookbook for individuals living on $4 a day. Another session, "You Still da Balm," taught participants how to make lotion and distill essential oils. Educational workshops brought participants together in community-based forums to reflect on new ways of thinking about Jewish life. "Shmeetup.com" explored fresh ways of thinking about the *Shmita* year – the year of letting the land go fallow specified in the biblical text of Leviticus; more on this below – in the twenty-first century. "Jewish Food Justice 101" told the story of the "tomato rabbis" who were involved with the Immokalee farmworkers movement.[13]

Coastal Roots has also housed a Sukkah design competition where participants were invited to reimagine the ancient temporary structure that is traditionally erected for one week each autumn to commemorate the holiday.[14] The Sukkah designs of three artists were selected by a panel of architects and designers that were then constructed by volunteers on the Ranch's property in the weeks leading up to the Sukkot celebration. The guidelines for a Sukkah were simple: "the structure must be temporary; it must have at least two-and-a-half walls; it must be big enough to contain a table and most of a person's body; and it must have a roof made of shade-providing organic materials through which a person can see the stars."[15] The reimagined Sukkahs served as center stage of the weeklong Sukkot on the Ranch celebration, accentuating the structure's religious and agro-ecological significance. As the farm's Rabbi, Andy Kastner put it: "The Sukkah's religious function is to honor the temporary structures that the Israelites resided in during their migration from Egypt... We're interested in exploring how this space can express and advance ideas of community engagement, social justice, and sustainability."[16]

Consider next an example of ritualization on the farm from The Abundant Table's "Sunday Farm Church." Originally a campus ministry of California State University, Abundant Table has evolved into an internship program for young adults where college aged students are educated to work on a local, sustainable farm, live in intentional community, and engage in social justice building in their community and through the farm church. Abundant Table's mission is to change lives and systems by creating sustainable relationships to the land and local community. "Born out of a recognition of the deep connection between our physical and spiritual needs," Abundant Table welcomes people from all perspectives and backgrounds, offering opportunities for various communities to "connect farm work, spirituality, and social justice within a progressive Judeo-Christian tradition."[17] They engage people from the wider community and the university in "a mission to transform our food system towards increased health for all people, while practicing responsible stewardship and connection to the earth."[18]

Abundant Table's weekly Farm Church, as with Coastal Roots' ceremonial events, is an interfaith and ecumenical endeavor that invites people of all faith traditions to explore spirituality and social justice work in connection with farm and food work. "Join us," Abundant Table states, "as we seek to discover a transforming faith through worship, study, community, food, farming, and service."[19] Held on Sunday evenings, Farm Church consists of a communal meal and worship service, which is held at a shared space such as the farmhouse, a church member's home, or another community venue. Representative of the services are announcements such as this one: "This week, we explore the Abundant Table's pillars of Celebration and Community. In weekdays filled with getting our hands dirty with the work of justice and love, Sundays serve as a Sabbath for many of us. We celebrate together by sharing good food, rejuvenating reflection and spiritual care. A counter-cultural weekly gathering where we slow to the world, affirm and lift up one another is the practice that gives many of us the strength to go on doing good work into the next week."[20]

Notice how acts of ritualization at these farm sites create spaces within spaces to demarcate and spotlight certain aspects of agricultural and religious practice. In one sense, intentional ritual activities such the building of the Sukkahs and enactment of Sunday Farm Church on farm property are set off and privileged as distinctively religious activities in relation to other secular ones surrounding it, including the rest of the week's day in and day out farming activities. In another sense, the farm space itself, and more generally the type of agriculture being practiced there, is viewed as having a type of secular symbolic meaning, in terms of its set-apartness from conventional, industrial forms of agriculture and eating. Both ways ritualization on the farm takes place not only through intentional habituated ceremonial practices, but also through the enactment of community-based, alternative agricultural activities themselves, which attempt to create things the way they ought to be in the face of the way they currently are. As Jonathan Z. Smith observes, "ritual is, above all, an assertion of difference . . . a means of performing the way things ought to be in conscious tension to the way things are" (as cited in Gould 2005, 63). In this way, the ritualization of agriculture and food practices may be interpreted as a form of "public witness" to the collective moral failure of industrial society – and a call to do better – to live respectfully and cooperatively with land. It may also function as a form of public witness to religious traditions, calling people of faith to live more deeply, justly, and joyfully in concert with other people and plants, animals and soil.[21]

It is this element of difference in ritual practice, between the way things are and the way things ought to be, that raises one of the difficult aspects of the ritualization of agricultural and food practices. Given that rituals explicitly or implicitly assert a difference between this way of living and that way of living, between this way of perceiving and that way of perceiving, between this way of practicing faithful devotion and that way of practicing faithful devotion they necessarily exclude those who do not understand, feel comfortable, or believe in performing this or that type of symbolic action – no matter how "high" or "low" the ritual activity may be. Some people, for instance, may insist that they do not need rituals to make meaning out of the agricultural and food process.[22] Additionally, the agriculturalization of central religious practices may raise suspicion among religionists who view them as overstepping theological bounds in ways that threaten tradition and community life. I say more below about some of these problematic dimensions. Before that, however, another element in the production of the sacred on religious farm sites warrants attention.

Reinterpretation on the farm

In many ways, the ritualization of agricultural and food activities is what makes faith-based farms explicitly religious, for different from their secular counterparts, faith-based farms that involve embodied ritual activities such as the ones just described explicitly and publically promote the notion that the agricultural and food process is a sacred activity that warrants attention as such. Yet faith-based farms may also be interpreted as sacred spaces for how they focus fundamental questions about what it means to be a human being in a meaningful world and for how they narrate the significance of certain types of environments and relationships. This includes reinterpretations about what it means to be a faithful person, and about what faithful practice entails. Of particular interest for this book's purpose are the hybridized ways in which religious farms perform these interpretive labors, for at times they are explicitly religious, drawing on ancient sacred texts and theological beliefs, while at other times they are intentionally secular, emphasizing ecological, social, or political elements.

Consider how Coastal Roots Farm interprets what it means to be a Jewish farm in relation to the broader culture of the San Diego region where it is located. From the beginning, Coastal Root's founders were interested in thinking about how religion, Jewish faith in particular, could meaningfully interact with regional public concerns. They did not "wake up one day and decide to buy a big farm," Kastner told me.[23] They began by doing some research about the area. In particular, they wanted to learn what inspired people, and what they felt was missing and needed in the region. Through focus group research with Jewish residents they found the following: Only 7 percent of the county's Jewish population was connected to a Jewish organization or institution (e.g., a school, synagogue, social organization, or community event). Seventy-five percent of married individuals were in inter-faith marriages. Even though the majority of Jewish residents in the region were not connected to a formal Jewish organization, they still wanted to connect their Jewish values with those of coastal California where they lived. They were inter-ested in health, spirituality, agriculture, and the environment, as well as connections to Israel.[24] A motif that emerged that was somewhat surprising, Kastner said, was that people wanted a community common space in addition to the beach.

The Ranch was born out of this spirit. Steeped deeply in Jewish agricultural tradition, the farm's activities nevertheless attempt to promote the idea that there is ancient wisdom related to food practices that can be universally accessed by Jews and non-Jews alike. This is reflected in the ways in which traditional Jewish festivals and rituals are repurposed in order to build community and transcend borders of religious faith. Ritualized events involve ceremonial activities that all participants, no matter their particular affiliation, can appreciate. Prior to Sukkot on the Ranch, for example, volunteers, Jewish and non-Jewish, gathered on the farm for a workday where fields were prepared for the *Shmita* year in the Jewish seasonal calendar. The *Shmita* year is a Jewish agricultural practice instituted in the sabbatical laws of the Hebrew Bible, where the Israelites were instructed to make a Sabbath for the land in which fields were let fallow every seven years as part of a cycle that focused on release, restoration, renewal, and a recentering of community-based values. There is no requirement outside of Israel for the performance of this ritual, the farm's man-ager Daron "Farmer D" Joffe told me, but Coastal Roots chose to incorporate and reinvent it as part of its commitment to connect ancient Jewish agricultural wisdom and biodynamic farming, both which accentuate the importance of seasonal cycles and the need for periods of revitalization.[25]

This *Shmita* workday at Coastal Roots volunteers helped to prune the vineyard and spread seeds of cover crops that would replenish soils over the winter. At the day's close there was an evening meal and celebratory blessing. A final ceremony drew on ancient texts and the framework of the *Havdalah* ritual, which is tradition-ally performed as a symbolic transition that marks the end of Shabbat and other Jewish holidays. Three elements mark the making of *Havdalah* (Hebrew for "to separate"): a cup of wine, a box of aromatic spices, and a multiwicked candle, each, when used in the ceremony, are accompanied by Hebrew blessings that signify various elements of separation and transition – sacred and profane, light and dark, spiritual and material. The *Havdalah* opens with the reading of a series of biblical verses, the candle is lit, the cup is lifted, the spice box is smelled, participants hold their hands to the candle's fire, and a final blessing is sung. This particular workday on the farm, the *Havdalah* was used to mark the transition from the sixth to the seventh year, the *Shmita* year, for which the farm was preparing. When the *Havdalah* candle was lit, a traditional Hebrew blessing was said, but now participants, who came from a variety of backgrounds, asked for vision, inspiration, and warmth – for themselves and for the farm. They wrote their wishes in marker on a piece of paper and buried them in the field as the final planting of year. Non-Jewish participants, said Kastner, enjoyed taking part in an ancient spiritual and agricultural rite, while Jewish participants appreciated connecting to their own heritage in a new way.[26]

Mother Carr's farm engages in similar interpretive work by reorienting central devotional practices in the context of public engagement with critical agricultural and food issues. In this case, The Church of God's sensibilities regarding evangelism and social outreach are retooled in light of community-based farming activities. As Williamson states: "The purpose of the farm is to move all people closer to God by showing his compassion…We send more than ten percent of our harvest to local food kitchens. We're able to give stipends to some workers and minister them back into society. It allows us to minister to people and talk to people about God and how he works in a physical form. Instead of just seeing us go to church, they see us in action."[27] The church's pastor, Reverend Jerald January further narrates the sacred mission of the farm, emphasizing how it allows the church community to follow God and minister to those in need: "The farm provides food the way the Lord intended – natural. However, it has proven God's intent in not only nutrition but also purpose for those men and women who find fulfillment in working the soil. There are numerous opportunities to tell curious folks about the plan God gave us to grow food and provide it at an affordable cost. In addition, we're able to give away a portion to homeless shelters and soup kitchens, giving glory to God."[28] Mother Carr's Farm operates a CSA where church and community members can purchase a whole or half-share of vegetables for 300 or 150 dollars a season. "It's helping people, who couldn't afford to eat quality, eat quality food," says Williamson.[29] Shareholders also receive honey from the beehives at the farm, which doubles as a monarch butterfly sanctuary. This believes Williamson "will help us to become an even healthier community and create better men and women of God."[30]

Note how in each of these accounts, reinterpretations of religious practices and beliefs involve the type of symbolic reordering of spatial environments and sets of relationships Chidester and Linenthal (1995) suggest as characteristic of the making of sacred space. For now, it is the agroecological environment – rather than the built environment of a church or synagogue – that becomes central to the enactment of sacred activity. Moreover, it is the network of relationships that are integral to the sustenance of farm and food justice activities that are elevated in terms of their sacred significance. Relationships among people, soil, plants, insects, water, and air are accentuated, as are relationships among religionists and the broader community, particularly people living at the margins of society. In these ways, farm sites are converted to sacred status not only for how they ritualize the agricultural process, but also for how they expand the boundaries of the moral community. In a trick of inversion, faithfulness is practiced not only through devotional acts performed indoors in a fabricated building in the company of other believers, but also through agricultural and food work enacted outdoors in the field or in the surrounding community in the company of many others.

Note too how theological and denominational differences play out on these farm sites. Coastal Root's progressive Jewish orientation and work with Hazon grounds it in a tradition that emphasizes social ecological change in the world and renewing the Jewish community.[31] Mother Carr's evangelical Protestant underpinnings focus on divine sovereignty and social witness, interpreting organic farming as a way to enact the "natural" ways of God's earth, serve others, and glorify God. Drawing on "a progressive Judeo-Christian tradition," Abundant Table spotlights connections between farm work and spirituality and social justice.[32]

The ritualization and reinterpretation that goes on in these farm spaces is for the most part viewed positively by participants and the larger faith community. Yet, there are also difficult dimensions embedded in these efforts to retool religious traditions in agricultural light. This is particularly apparent where farm activities explicitly or implicitly challenge received assumptions related to conventional religious and agricultural practices. Thus, we turn in the next and final section to consider some of the contested aspects of these religious farm sites, for here too the sacred is being produced, in this case, through activities marked by conflict and negotiation.

Contest on the farm

Part of Coastal Roots Farm's food activities involves a training program for Jewish young adults in social environmental activism. A 15 -month fellowship, the Jewish Food Justice Fellowship program is longer than most agriculture and food training programs for young professionals. This is because Coastal Roots hopes to give new activists enough time to become skilled in the areas of nonprofit organizing and leadership so they can eventually contribute in significant ways to the development of the Jewish environmental movement. By becoming what Kastner calls "a leadership pipeline for millenials," Coastal also wants to support the food justice work of San Diego's north county. Reputable Jewish farms such as Adamah in Falls Creek, Connecticut and Urban Adamah in Berkeley, California give Jewish youth and young adults immersive experiences where they learn homesteading and farming skills. Coastal Roots wanted to add to this work by engaging young Jewish food activists in "robust professional development," said Kastner. Working with the fellows to build hard and soft skills related to nonproject leadership, the Food Justice Fellowship program focuses on building grant-writing and communication capacities, as well as hands-on practical experiences with community-based food efforts. Three days a week fellows work in non-Jewish, nonprofit organizations, and two days they work in Jewish schools and organizations with farm to school programs and public policy advocacy efforts.

The Food Justice Fellowship strives to create a notion of Jewish activism that extends beyond traditional understandings about what it means to be Jewish in America. Jewishness exists in the synagogue and yeshiva, yes – but it also goes beyond this, said Kastner. What they want the fellows to understand is that one can activate Jewishness by doing good and by doing justice in the world. Jewishness is not something owned only by the Jews, but a universally applicable wisdom, Kastner wants the fellows to learn. For most of the fellows, he said, this idea presents a steep learning curve, mostly because it requires breaching embedded boundaries related to Jewish identity and religiousness.

Coastal Roots work involves additional contested elements, including those related to land use. Zoning laws in San Diego County prohibit the practice of religious worship on agriculturally zoned land, which is how Coastal Roots is designated. Still, the Ranch involves a variety of Jewish-based ceremonial activities: Sukkot on the Ranch, the vineyard workday, *Shmita* prep-day. The way they get around the zoning issue is that they avoid the celebration of high holy services on site. This is not only for political purposes, said Kastner, but also for theological ones. Coastal Roots, he said, does not want to be a synagogue with a tractor. What they want to be is a farm community that is enacting Jewish agricultural wisdom in a way that blends ancient and regional cultural knowledge that is universally accessible to the broader public, Jewish and non-Jewish.

The zoning laws do not prohibit the type of ceremonial activities they are performing, Kastner told me. Nevertheless, they want to be careful in their approach. So Coastal Roots Farm is applying the philosophy of permaculture to their social location. The agricultural method of permaculture advises observation of the land and its seasons for at least a year before planting. Similarly, Kastner said, they are attempting to observe the area, including the zoning laws and the culture of the place, as they enter the process of developing the farm. They want to be "super consistent" with what they are offering, Kastner stated, which means they are prudent when it comes to enacting this or that type of activity, religious or agricultural.

Mother Carr's farm too has experienced contested elements over land use, though, in this case related to agricultural method and landscape design. The farm, Williamson told me, is a "real farm," on "real farmland."[33] But it does not look like what people expect a farm to look, he said. "It looks messy." And some parishioners do not like the look of a messy farm. So much so that some of the church's congregants, including a former farmer, have tried to convince Williamson to go conventional, plant round-up ready corn, use chemical fertilizers and herbicides. But Williamson says he wants to "keep it natural." What he is trying to do is build something durable, something that is going to last a long time. For the most part, convincing church members of the organic farm's methods and benefits has been relatively easy, Williamson told me. In the first year their CSA sold over a hundred shares, and they were able to donate vegetables to a community food pantry as well.

It has, nevertheless, not always been easy to recruit parishioners to work on the farm. Mt. Vernon is a black church, and some members still associate working in the fields with slave labor, Williamson said. Additionally, the disconnection of people from the agricultural and food process has at times generated skepticism and apathy among congregants about the church's farm activities. Most people of this generation, the farm intern Mark told me, do not know where to begin when it comes to planting or harvesting food, which at times keeps them from becoming involved. Williamson has observed that that once people actually get out on the farm and learn that they can contribute in a variety of ways – from picking and sorting vegetables to weeding to working CSA share distribution days – minds are slowly changed. Volunteers also experience the beauty and vitality of the farm site, another aspect of educating the congregation about the project's value. Even the pastor, Williamson told me, has begun to incorporate agricultural metaphors in his sermons.

A final example of the contested dimensions of the production of sacred farm spaces comes from Abundant Table. In the fall of 2014, there was a chemical spill in Santa Paula, which is approximately a mile away from the farm site. Abundant Table was subsequently shut down for nearly four weeks as soil tests were completed to determine whether the fields and produce had been contaminated. Officials estimated that the explosion leached hazardous chemical residue a square mile from the spill site. With the farm lying just at the border of that mile marker, there was significant uncertainty as to whether Abundant Table's land had been affected, and if so, to what extent. The fields were full of produce, waiting to be harvested, but for weeks, farm staff was not allowed onto the site as they waited to receive results from the tests.

In the end, it was determined that the farm's land had been unaffected by the chemical drift from the spill. Yet the fact that the farm site *could have* been contaminated, or, in symbolic terms, *desecrated,* heightened the meaning of the space's significance. This is particularly apparent in the reflections written by farm staff and CSA members in the weeks following the spill. In one response, Farm Church coordinators stated: "We at *The Abundant Table / Join the Farm* are all still processing the tangled and messy web of relationships that emerged in the aftermath of the spill, and striving to see where our place in it all is. I hope that we will get to hear from different members of our organization, or even possibly from YOU!, as we continue to meditate on and dialogue about the realities of our place in this very industrial and complex world."[34] A farm intern emphasized the joyous experience of being allowed back on the farm after the fear of contamination had been dispelled by news that the site was unaffected and safe for harvest:

> I am ecstatically back to writing a correspondence after a nearly 4-week long hiatus from CSA deliveries while we waited to receive confirmation that our farm was unaffected by the Santa Paula chemical spill on November 18th. Having received results that indicated our fields were fully safe to harvest from, we are back in the rows and marveling at how much we've missed eating, touching, and harvesting the produce in the last month. It was with much jumping and shouts of "hurrah!" that your farm team received the good news that we could consciably re-start harvests for the CSA program, and for the kids in the Ventura and Conejo Valley Unified School Districts this week. Every beet pulled out of the ground has been a thrill; every bursting tomato plucked from the vine, a joy.[35]

Notice how both statements juxtapose the practices of community-based farming with those of broader industrial culture. Not only did the threat of desecration accentuate the farm's significance and meaning for participants, it spotlighted the "realities" they faced in light of "this very industrial and complex world." By suggesting that these are realities that cannot ultimately be escaped or avoided, religious farms represent the notion that the sacred can never be in practice "purely" separated from the profane.

Even as the contested character of these religious farm sites may not be as pronounced as other types of sacred spaces in America, they are, I would argue, generating novel forms spirituality that over time may cause increasing consternation among religionists insofar as they challenge conventional forms of faithful practice. Furthermore, the type of alternative community-based agriculture that these farms practice is often understood by participants as a form of counter-(agri)cultural resistance to the industrial food system. As agricultural and food issues become more pronounced in public deliberation about how to respond to global and local pressures posed by climate change and social inequities, debates about food systems will likely become further entrenched, potentially making sacred farms sources of greater scrutiny and contestation.[36]

The food and faith movement is a relatively recent phenomenon, with the sacred quality of farm spaces and the agroecologization of religious traditions and communities in flux. As emergent forms of spiritual practice in America, new religious farm sites remain in a transitional phase where they are in the process of defining, in the terms of their respective traditions and regional food cultures, what is meant by sacred food and agriculture, and therefore, what is meant by sacred land, in light of current social ecological problems. Despite this, these farms speak well to a hybridized view of the sacred, where multiple values – aesthetic, spiritual, moral, ecological, economic, and political – intermingle and overlap to create expanded meanings for agriculture, food, and religion. They should be considered sacred spaces for how they ritualize the agricultural and food process and produce reinterpretations of what it means to be human in relation to the wider land and human community. Furthermore, sacred farm sites should not go overlooked in the study of agricultural and food ethics and religion and ecology, for they provide interesting test cases for how religious narratives are being "worked into" larger cultural conversations about the ethics of agriculture and food, as well as for how environmental practices are being "worked into" the spiritual practices of religious communities.

Notes

1 See Mother Carr's Organic Farm website, http://mothercarrorganicfarm.org/ (accessed December 20, 2014).
2 The farms were selected based on recommendations made to me by leading practitioners and scholars working in the food and faith movement. They were also selected for their variety in terms of how they represent different denominations and faith traditions in America.
3 Coastal Roots Farm is a program sponsored by the Leichtag Foundation and is located in Leichtag Commons, which also hosts Jewish-based educational and community programs on self-sufficiency and other social entrepreneurial ventures. See https://leichtag.org/commons/ (accessed October 28, 2017).

4 See The Abundant Table website, http://theabundanttable.org/ (accessed January 7, 2015).

5 See Mother Carr's Organic Farm webpage: http://vpcog.org/mother-carrs-organic-farm (accessed February 19, 2015).

6 For more on the notion of environmental spirituality see Gretel Van Wieren, *Restored to Earth: Christianity, Environmental Ethics, and Ecological Restoration* (Georgetown University Press, 2013), 91–94.

7 On the universal experience of eating, see Leon Kass' *The Hungry Soul: Eating and the Perfecting of Our Nature* (New York: The Free Press, 1994).

8 For the discussion that follows, I am indebted to David Chidester and Edward T. Linenthal's Introduction in their edited volume, *American Sacred Space* (Bloomington and Indianapolis, IN: Indiana University Press, 1995), 1–42.

9 Drawing on van der Leeuw's classic study of the phenomenology of religion, *Religion in Essence and Manifestation*, Chidester and Linenthal (1995) underline four aspects of a politics of sacred space that they view as especially important: 1) the positioning of a sacred place is a "political act" that involves the conquest of space; 2) there is "politics of property" with sacred space that "can be asserted and maintained through claims and counter-claims on its ownership"; 3) the construction of sacred space is marked by the negotiation of relationships whereby some persons are "left out, kept out, or forced out," in other words, by "a politics of exclusion"; and 4) a "politics of exile" is the context that characterizes sacred space in the modern age, for in today's age, different from a more "primitive" or "peasant" past, people are so alienated from the sacred that the most sacred places are "remote," with the most authentic religious experiences marked by a certain feeling of homesickness for these places. See Chidester and Linenthal (1995, 7–9).

10 Chidester and Linenthal here follow Michel Foucault's insistence that any exercise of power fundamentally involves space. See Michel Foucault, "Space, Knowledge, and Power," in Paul Rabinow, ed., *The Foucault Reader* (New York: Pantheon, 1984), 252. See Foucault, "Questions of Geography," in Colin Gordon, ed., *Power/Knowledge: Selected Interviews and Other Writings 1972–1977* (New York: Pantheon, 1980), 63–77; cited in Chidester and Linenthal (1995, 15).

11 Catherine Bell uses the term "ritualization" over "ritual" given the former concept's attention to the active process that occurs when people privilege one type of activity over and against another. See her *Ritual Theory, Ritual Practice* (1992, 32–35).

12 Rebecca Gould makes a similar point in relation to homesteading in her *At Home in Nature: Modern Homesteading and Spiritual Practice in America* (2005, 63–101). Drawing on Gould's work, I have interpreted ecological restoration as a form of spiritual practice in my book *Restored to Earth: Christianity, Ecological Restoration* (2013).

13 See Sukkot on the Ranch schedule, http://jewishnorthcounty.com/sukkotattheranch/schedule/ (accessed February 19, 2015).

14 See the Jewish Coastal North County website, http://jewishnorthcounty.com/sukkotat-theranch/ (accessed January 7, 2014).

15 See the announcement for the Sukkot design competition, http://www.leichtag.org/2014/07/announcing-sukkot-ranch-design-competition/ (accessed December 7, 2015).

16 Ibid.

17 See The Abundant Table website, http://theabundanttable.org/ (accessed January 7, 2015).

18 Ibid.

19 See The Abundant Table website, "Farm Church," http://theabundanttable.org/farm-to-faith/farmchurch/ (accessed January 7, 2015).

20 See The Abundant Table website, "Field Journal," http://theabundanttable.org/2014/12/advent-four-community-and-celebration/#more-%27 (accessed January 30, 2015).

21 For more on the idea of environmental action as a form of public witness, see Van Wieren, *Restored to Earth* (2013, 253–9).

22 This type of argument has been made in relation to the ritualization of ecological restoration practice. See, for example, Dwight Baldwin, Judith De Luce, and Carl Pletsch's *Beyond Preservation: Restoring and Inventing Landscapes* (1993).

23 Personal communication, December 9, 2014.

24 See "Report to the Leichtag Foundation: Jewish Life in North County, San Diego, Focus Group Executive Summary," http://www.leichtag.org/wp-content/uploads/ 2014/02/5-12-Leichtag-Foundation-Focus-Groups-Exec-Summary-FINAL.pdf (accessed February 19, 2015).

25 As already noted in Chapter 2, the method of biodynamic farming comes from the work of Austrian philosopher and scientist, Rudolf Steiner, who is most well known for founding the Waldorf education system. For more on Steiner and his connection to biodynamic farming see Daron "Farm D" Joffe's *Citizen Farmers: The Biodynamic Way to Grow Healthy Food, Build Thriving Communities, and Give back to the Earth* (2014). Joffe defines biodynamic agriculture as "a type of organic farming that treats the farm as a self-contained living organism that can provide everything it needs from within. It is a closed-loop sustainable approach to agriculture that focuses on growing plants, feeding animals, making compost, and replenishing the soil. Repeating this cycle creates a regenerative process that improves the fertility of the farm over time rather than depleting it. Biodynamic farmers also apply homeopathic medicine to the earth by making special preparations to further enhance the quality of the soil, crops, and animals they produce" (Joffe 2014, 14). For more on Steiner's metaphysic of the natural world, see Bron Taylor's *Dark Green Religion: Nature Spirituality and the Planetary Future* (2009, 156–7).

26 Personal communication, December 9, 2014.

27 Church of God News (CHOG) website, http://chognews.org/2014/07/25/mother-carrs-organic-farm-harvesting-hope-in-chicago/ (accessed, January 8, 2015).

28 Ibid.

29 Ibid.

30 Ibid.

31 For more on Hazon's values and beliefs, see http://hazon.org/about/theory-of-change/ (accessed December 7, 2015).

32 See "Farm to Faith," http://theabundanttable.org/farm-to-faith/ (accessed December 7, 2015).

33 Personal communication, September 18, 2014.

34 See The Abundant Table website, "Field Journal," http://theabundanttable.org/2014/ 12/reflections-on-community-supported-agriculture-csa/#more-%27 (accessed January 30, 2015).

35 Ibid.

36 For an example of this already occurring in public discourse, see the work of the organization, Truth in Food, which strongly critiques environmentally oriented religious practices, particularly those related to food. See an essay on the Truth in Food website, "Earth is Great; Earth is Good; Let us Thank Her for our Food," http://truthinfood.com/index. php?option=com_content&view=article&id=90:churches-and-new-food-morality&ca tid=10:previousissues&Itemid=2 (accessed February 13, 2015).

References

Baldwin, D., De Luce, J., and Pletsch, C. eds. (1993) *Beyond Preservation: Restoring and Inventing Landscapes*, University of Minnesota Press, Minneapolis, MN.

Bell, C. (1992) *Ritual Theory, Ritual Practice*, Oxford University Press, Oxford.

Chidester, D. and Linenthal, E. eds. (1995) "Introduction," *American Sacred Space*, Indiana University Press, IN.

Joffe, D. (with Puckett, S.) (2014) *Citizen Farmers: The Biodynamic Way to Grow Healthy Food, Build Thriving Communities, and Give back to the Earth*, Steward, Tabori, & Chang, New York, NY.

Kass, L. (1994) *The Hungry Soul: Eating and the Perfecting of Our Nature*, The Free Press, New York, NY.

Taylor, B. (2009) *Dark Green Religion: Nature Spirituality and the Planetary Future*, University of California Press, Berkeley, CA.

Van Wieren, G. (2013) *Restored to Earth: Christianity, Environmental Ethics, and Ecological Restoration*, Georgetown University Press, Washington DC.

Van Wieren, G. (2017) "The New Sacred Farm," *Worldviews: Global Religions, Cultures, and Ecology*, 21(2), 113–33.

INDEX

The 2007/8 Human Development Report: Fighting Climate Change: Human Solidarity in a Divided World 100

Abdul-Matin, Ibrahim 72–5
Abrahamic traditions 3
Abundant Table 45, 114, 117, 123
abuse, animals 67–70
AFHVS (Agriculture Food and Human Values Society) 4
agrarian agriculture 27–8
agrarian meat eating 70–2
agrarian philosophies 5
The Agrarian Vision: Sustainability and Environmental Ethics (Thompson) 5
agricultural and food ethics 9–12
agriculture 36; anthropocentric Christianity and mechanized agriculture 24–6; eating in exile 28–30; impacts on climate 97–101; industrial versus restorative 15; restorative agriculture 31; sustainable agriculture 38–45; water *see* water; *see also* farming
Agriculture and Human Values 4
Agriculture Food and Human Values Society (AFHVS) 4
AgriProcessors 67–8
Albo, Josheph 69
al-Hayani, Fatima Agha 53–4
Alliance of Religions and Conservation (ARC) 108–10
animal ethicists 64–5
animal production 65–7, 98–9

animal welfare 4, 8, 64, 67–70
animals 64; agrarian meat eating 70–2; humane subject 67–70; Norwich Meadows Farm 77–8; Ryan's Retreat 75–7; *see also* meat eating
Anthropocentric Christianity, mechanized agriculture 24–6
aquifers 82–3
ARC (Alliance of Religions and Conservation) 108–10
Archer Daniels Midland 99
ascendancy, animals 68–9
Ault, Colorado 89
Ayers, Jennifer 8–9

Backyard to Table 60–1
Bailey, Liberty Hyde, spiritual science of agriculture 41–2
Balaram 7
Barlow, Maude 83–4, 86–7
Bechtel Corporation 88
Bell, Catherine 115
Berry, Wendell 1, 9–10, 26–8, 36
biodiversity 67, 101
Bolivia, water 88
Bonhoeffer, Dietrich 30
Borgmann, Albert 5
Borlaug, Norman 52
Brown, Lester 81–2
Brown, Sister Joan 91
Bt. Corn 49
Buiter, Willem 87
buy and dry 88

CAFOs (Concentrated Animal Feeding
    Operations) 66, 98
Callicott, J. Baird 64
Calvin, John 1
Cargill 99
Carr, Mother Julia 112
Carson, Rachel 1, 2
Carver, George Washington 42–5
Catholic Worker 7
Catholicism: climate change 102–4; GMOs
    (genetically modified organisms) 54
chemical biotechnologies 1
Cheshvan 58–9
Chidester, David 114–15, 120
children, water pollution 86
Christianity: creation 71; Evangelical
    Climate Initiative 104–5; meat eating
    70–2; mechanized agriculture 24–6;
    water 89–92
climate, agricultural impacts on 97–101
climate change, religion 101–10
Coastal Roots Farm 45, 114, 116; contested
    elements 121–4; reinterpretation 118–20
Cochabamba, Bolivia 88
comparative religious environmental
    ethics 14–15
Concentrated Animal Feeding Operations
    (CAFOs) 66, 98
contested elements, on farms 121–4
conventional agriculture 15
corporate control, GMOs (genetically
    modified organisms) 52
creation, Christianity 71
cultivar 41

dark green religion 45
Day, Dorothy 6–7
de Chardin, Theilhard 7
dead zones 84–5
debate over GMOs 48–53
Derrida, Jacques 68–9
desecrated soil 36–8
Dirt 34
dirt, defining 34–6
Dominican Sisters 57–8
Dresner, Rabbi Samuel 69

ecological diseases, farming 21–4
ecological health, GMOs (genetically
    modified organisms) 49–50
ecology/nature 14
Eighth Day Farm 60
ELCA (Evangelical Lutheran Church of
    America) 114
"The Eleventh Commandment" 36–7

Eliade, Mircea 114
Emerson, Ralph Waldo 34
environmental ethics 2; agricultural and
    food ethics 9–12; animal production
    65–6; philosophical environmental ethics
    and food 3–6; religious environmental
    ethics and food 6–9
environmental issues 2
environmental justice philosophers 5
Episcopal Church 114
ethical issues 2
ethics: defined 13–14; environmental ethics
    2; food ethics 2
European Society of Agricultural and Food
    Ethics (EURSafe) 4
Evangelical Climate Initiative 104–5
Evangelical Lutheran Church of America
    (ELCA) 114
exile, eating in 28–30

Faith in Place 91
fall of Adam and Eve 29–30
FAO/UNEP (Food and Agriculture
    Organization/United Nation
    Environment Programme) 37, 50
Farb, Joann 49–50, 56
Farmer D (Daron Joffe) 60, 119
farming 10; bad versus good 26–8;
    eating in exile 28–30; as an ecological
    disease 21–4
Farming God's Way 108–10
farms: Abundant Table 45, 114, 117, 123;
    Coastal Roots Farm 45, 114, 116;
    contested elements 121–4; Genesis Farm
    57–8, 60–1; Leichtag Ranch 59; Mother
    Carr's Organic Farm 45, 112–13;
    reinterpretation 118–21; ritualization
    115–18; sacred spaces 114–15
Ferrell, John S. 42
Filthaut, Sister Jeannette 59
focal practices 5
Foltz, Richard 8, 72
food: agricultural and food ethics 9–12;
    comparative religious environmental
    ethics 14–15; eating in exile 28–30;
    philosophical environmental ethics and
    3–6; religious environmental ethics 6–9
Food and Agriculture Organization/United
    Nation Environment Programme
    (FAO/UNEP) 37
food and faith movement 2–3
food ethics 2
food justice 5–6
Food Justice Fellowship 121
food justice studies 5

food system disorders 7
Foreman, Dave 22
Foucault, Michel 115
Francis, Saint of Assisi 26
From Field to Fork: Food Ethics for Everyone
(Thompson) 5

garden communes 7
GATT (General Agreement on Tariffs and
Trade) 51
Gaud, William 1
General Agreement on Tariffs and Trade
(GATT) 51
Genesis Farm 57–8, 60–1
genetically modified organisms (GMOs) 2,
48; debate over 48–53; religion 53–7
Gerritsen, Jim 60
Gevirtz, Rabbi Elihu 56
Glennon, Robert 83
global hunger 6
global population, feeding with
GMOs 50–1
global warming, animal production 66
global warming potential (GWP) 66
GMOs (genetically modified organisms)
2, 48; debate over 48–53; religion
53–7
good death 70
Gottlieb, Robert 6
Green Revolution 1, 51
green zabiha 72–5
Greenberg, Paul 85
GreenFaith 89–91
greenhouse gas emissions 97–8
Grim, John 13
Gross, Aaron 67–70
groundwater 82–3
GWP (global warming potential) 66

halal 74
ha-Nasi, Judah 69
Haynes, Richard 4
Hazon 58–9, 114
heirloom seeds 60
heterotopia 115
Hillel, Daniel 35
The Holy Earth (Bailey) 41–2
Holy Family Catholic Church 92
Hopkins, Gerard Manley 28
hospitality houses 7
Howard, Phillip 52
Howard, Sir Albert 10–11
human health, GMOs (genetically modified
organisms) 49–50
humane subject 67–70

hunger ethics 4, 6
hybridization 115

ICTSD (International Centre for Trade and
Sustainable Development) 100
IFANCA (Islamic Food and Nutrition
Council of America) 54
IMF (International Monetary Fund) 87
industrial agriculture, versus restorative
agriculture 15
industrial farming 26–8
inshallah 109
integral ecology 103
intellectual property rights 2; GMOs
(genetically modified organisms) 51–3
International Centre for Trade and
Sustainable Development (ICTSD) 100
International Monetary Fund (IMF) 87
International Panel on Climate Change
(IPCC) 97
inversion 120
IPCC (International Panel on Climate
Change) 97
IPRs (intellectual property rights) 2; GMOs
(genetically modified organisms) 51–3
Islam: climate change 105–7; Farming
God's Way 108–10; GMOs (genetically
modified organisms) 53–4, 56; meat
eating 72–5; nature 33; Norwich
Meadows Farm 77–8; Ramadan 91;
water 89–92
Islamic Declaration on Global Climate
Change 105–7
Islamic farming 109–10
Islamic food and Nutrition Council of
America (IFANCA) 54

Jackson, Wes 11–12, 107–8
January, Reverend Jerald 120
Joffe, Daron (Farmer D) 59, 60, 119
Joshi, Anupama 6
*The Journal of Agricultural and Environmental
Ethics* 4
Judaism: animals 69; GMOs (genetically
modified organisms) 53, 55, 56; seeds as
metaphors 58–9; water 89–92
Jung, Shannon L. 7

Kastner, Andy 116, 118–22
Kellogg, Charles 35–6
Kernza 108
Khan, Faraz 73
kilayim 53, 55
kindness, animals 69
Kirschenmann, Fred 38

Know Soil, Know Life 34–5
Kurdieh, Haifa 77
Kurdieh, Zaid 77

land conversion 66
land grab 65
Land Institute 11
The Land Institute 107–8
Lappé, Anna 97–8
Lappé, Francis Moore 1
Laudato Si' 102–4
Leichtag Ranch 59
Leopold, Aldo 2, 12, 35, 114
Linenthal, Edward T. 114–15, 120
Linzey, Andrew 8, 70
lived religion 57
lived theology 57
livestock production 65–7; water 82–4
Livestock's Long Shadow 67
Logan, William Bryant 34
Lowdermilk, Walter 22, 36–8

MacGillis, Miriam 57–8
Machane Yehuda 116
Man in the Landscape: A Historic View of the Esthetics of Nature (Shepard) 22
manageable risk 54
Martino, Cardinal Renato 54
Mason, Jim 4, 49, 50
Masri, Basheer Ahmad 72–3
Maurin, Peter 6–7
McDonagh, Sean 55
meat eating 64–7; agrarian meat eating 70–2; humane subject 67–70; Islam 72–5; Ramadan 91
mechanized agriculture, Anthropocentric Christianity and 24–6
meditation, spiritual science of agriculture 40
methane 66
Milgrom, Jacob 70
MNCs (multinational corporations) 51
Monsanto 52, 58, 60, 87
Moosa, Ebrahim 54
morality, defined 13–14
Mother Carr's Organic Farm 45, 112–13, 120; contested elements 122–3
multinational corporations (MNCs) 51
Muslim GreenWorship 91

Nana, Mufti Shaykh Abdullah 74
narratives of sacred seeds 57–61
Natural Systems Agriculture (NSA) 107–8
Navdanya 11
New Roots for Agriculture 12

Norwich Meadows Farm 77–8
NSA (Natural Systems Agriculture) 107–8

Obama, Senator Barack 68
Odaawaa 93
Ogallah Aquifer 83
On Care for our Common Home (Pope Francis) 54–5, 102–4
O'Neil, Onora 4
Organic Seed Growers and Trade Association (OSGATA) 58, 60
Özdemir, Ibrahim 33

palm production 99
Parvaiz, Mohammad Aslam 56
Peppard, Christiana 81–3, 85
Peterson, Anna 8
philosophical environmental ethics and food 3–6
Pimentel, David 37, 107
plants: GMOs (genetically modified organisms) 48–57; seeds 57–61
Plaster Creek, restoring 92–4
Plaster Creek Stewards 92–4
Pleistocene paradigm 22–4
Pollan, Michael 65
Pope Francis 54–5; climate change 102–4
privatizing water 87–8

Rabalais, Nancy 85
Ramadan 91
Rashi 69
reinterpretation, farms 118–21
religion: Christianity *see* Christianity; climate change 101–10; defined 13; GMOs (genetically modified organisms) 53–7; Islam *see* Islam; Judaism *see* Judaism; water 89–92; Zen Buddhism 26
religious ecology 13
religious environmental ethics, food and 6–9
restorative agriculture 31; versus industrial agriculture 15
restoring: Plaster Creek 92–4; sacred water 89–92; soil 38
ritualization 115–18
Roessing, Jeff 60
Roessing, Melissa 60
Rolston, III, Holmes 64
Roman Catholic Church, GMOs (genetically modified organisms) 54
Roof, Wade Clark 13
Ruffin, Kimberly 44
Rule of Benedict 1

Ryan, Nancy 75–7
Ryan, Will 75–7
Ryan's Retreat 75–7

sacred spaces 114–15
sacred water, restoring 89–92
Safran, Jonathan 68
Saint Francis of Assisi 26
Sanford, Whitney 7–8
Sauer, Carl 22
Schröer, Karl Julius 39
seed patenting, GMOs (genetically
    modified organisms) 51–3
seeds, narratives of sacred seeds 57–61
Seedy Saturdays 59–60
Shafran, Avi 69
Shepard, Paul 22–4
Shipley, John 91
Shiva, Vandana 10–11, 26–8, 51, 52, 87–8
Silent Spring (Carson) 1
Silver, Lee 50
Simon, Arthur 6
Singer, Peter 4, 49, 50, 64
Sisters of Providence of St. Vincent de
    Paul 59–60
Smil, Vaclav 50
Smith, Johnathan Z. 114, 117
social change, seeds 60–1
soil 33–6; desecrated soil 36–8; restoring 38;
    spirituality 45–6
Soil Science Society of America (SSSA) 34
South Valley, New Mexico 91
South Valley San Isidro celebration 91–2
*The Spirit of the Soil: Agriculture and
    Environmental Ethics* (Thompson) 4
spiritual dimensions of sustainable
    agriculture 38–45
spirituality 13; soil and 45–6
SSSA (Soil Science Society of America) 34
Steiner, Rudolf 39–40
Sukkot 116
Sukkot on the Ranch, Coastal Roots
    Farm 116
sustainable agriculture 38–45
sustainable development 81

Taittiriya Upanishad 11
taqwa 109
tawakkul 109

tawba 109
Tayeb 74
Taylor, Bron 13, 45
Technology Use Agreements (TUAs) 52
Thompson, Paul B. 4–5, 33, 36
tillage methods 25–6
Tlili, Sarra 8
trading water 88–9
Trinitarian thought 70
trinitas 70
TUAs (Technology Use Agreements) 52
Tucker, Mary Evelyn 13

UNDESA (United Nations Department of
    Economic and Social Affairs) 84
Unger, Peter 4
United States, water rights 88

Vallentyne, John R. 85
Vernon Park Church of God 112
von Balthasar, Hans Urs 70

Waskow, Rabbi Arthur 56
water 81–3; animal production
    66; degradation of 83–5; Plaster
    Creek, restoring 92–4; privatizing
    87–8; restoring sacred water 89–92;
    trading 88–9
water pollution 85–7
water rights 88
Water Shield 89–91
White, Lynn Jr. 24–6
Whitman, Walt 33
Whole Earth Meats 91
Williamson, Anthony 112, 120, 122–3
Wirzba, Norman 7, 28–30, 56, 70–2
W.K. Kellog Foundation 4
Wolff, Rabbi Akiva 53
women, water pollution 86
The World Bank 87–8
The World Council of Churches,
    GMOs (genetically modified
    organisms) 56–7
World Trade Organization (WTO) 51
wudu 91

Zabiha 74
Zen Buddhism 26
Zoloth, Laurie 55